BERLIN DEKO

BERLIN DEKO

Central European Furniture
from 1910 to 1930

Markus Winter & Don Freeman

arnoldsche

TABLE OF CONTENTS

1 Joseph Maria Olbrich (December 22, 1867–August 8, 1908), ladies' salon for the 300th anniversary of the city of Mannheim, Macassar ebony, manufactured by Julius Glückert, Darmstadt, 1907, Museum für Kunst und Kulturgeschichte, Dortmund

INTRODUCTION

Markus Winter

In his text on the work of the two architects Joseph Maria Olbrich (1867–1908) and Alfred Messel (1853–1909), published in October 1909, Leo Nachtlicht (1872–1942) stated:

"Messel scanned the past with a critical eye, Olbrich looked straight ahead with a vision into the distance. The former coordinated his architecture with a reverent conscientiousness, the latter gave birth to it out of himself. [...] Olbrich first looked within himself, unconcerned about what lay behind him, and then forward into an indeterminate mystical distance, to whose dark expanses only the light of his spirit led him. [...] We can count ourselves lucky to be living in this time."[1]

The results of these creative processes call into question the concept of separating tradition and modernity. They are furnishings that document an intensive search by their creators in sources—whether in the vastness of the Milky Way or in the roots of Germanic traditions—that have yet to be presented in sufficient detail. *Berlin Deko* documents a synthesis of modernity, tradition, mechanical production, and craftsmanship of often unpublished pieces of furniture and lighting fixtures.

The term "modern" is generally used to denote a concept that should be seen as distinct from the past; however, the more we try to distance ourselves from a particular concept, the closer we find

2   Terracotta kernos (vase for multiple offerings), terracotta, Cycladic, circa 2300–1900 BCE, The Metropolitan Museum of Art, New York

3   Hans Poelzig (April 30, 1869–June 14, 1936), large candelabra, ceramic, manufactured by Aelteste Volkstedter Porzellanmanufaktur, circa 1920, Deutsche Kunst und Dekoration, 1921

---

[1]   Leo Nachtlicht, Olbrich und Messel, in: Velhagen & Klasings Monatshefte, vol. 24, issue 2, October 1909, p. 201.

4   Film still, *The Golem: How He Came into the World*
set design: Hans Poelzig, 1920

ourselves to it. It is therefore not surprising when archaeologists, in their search for ancient and archaic cultures, unearth forms and shapes that seem futuristic. To better understand this phenomenon, it may be useful to broaden the perspective and examine the cosmic cycles as theorized by Plato[2] (circa 428–348 BCE) or Rudolf Steiner[3] (1861–1925). The Platonic Year, also known as the Great Year, is a cycle of 25,920 years in which the equinoxes complete a full precession through the zodiac. Plato associated this cycle with the return of cosmic harmony. Rudolf Steiner's system of time includes anthroposophical epochs or cultural ages, a framework linked to spiritual evolution. He proposed a system of epochs within a period of about 21,000 years. In this context, the traditional styles of Baroque and Rococo can be seen as relatively new and modern. Architect Hans Poelzig (1869–1936) drew on these styles to express emotion in his work.

In astrology, each planetary cycle begins with a "conjunction," where the planets line up at the same point in the zodiac. This marks the end of one phase and the beginning of a new one. As the planets move apart, they go through a series of aspects, with the opposition marking a key moment of full expression or realization. Between 1906 and 1910 Neptune and Uranus were in opposition. This was the climax of a cycle that began in 1821 and ended in 1993. A general interpretation of this aspect could be that there are differences or disagreements that need to be resolved. Uranus, the god of the sky, and Neptune, the god of the sea, show "imagination, aspiration and genius pull from the front, and lies, avoidances and fears drag it back—and somewhere in the middle there is the median point of real human evolution."[4]

An illustration of the change in style in the period around 1821 is given by a quote from Karl Friedrich

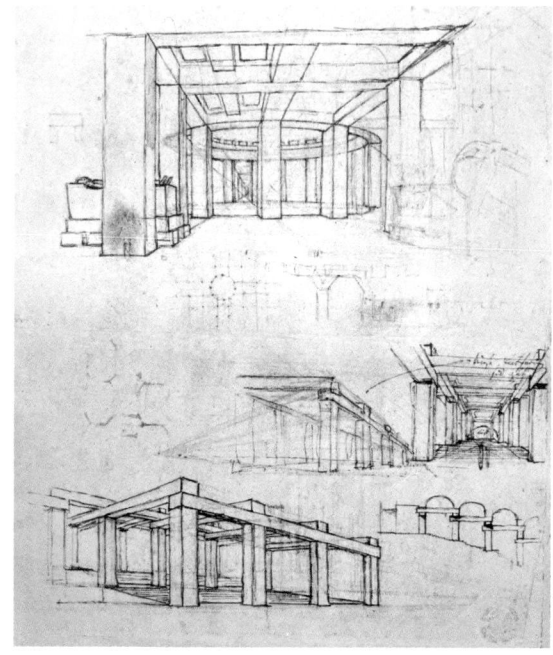

5   Friedrich Gilly (February 16, 1772–August 3, 1800), design for a mausoleum, circa 1798, TU Berlin, missing

Schinkel (1781–1841). In his diary he writes: "Very soon I fell into the error of purely radical abstraction, where I developed the entire conception for a particular work of architecture from its immediate trivial purpose alone and from its construction. In this case, something dry and rigid emerged that lacked freedom and completely excluded two essential elements, the historical and the poetic."[5] Schinkel and his teacher Friedrich Gilly (1772–1800) both had a notable influence on the works of Oskar Kaufmann (1873–1956), Bruno Paul (1874–1968) and Ludwig Mies van der Rohe (1886–1969).

Gilly's Design for a Mausoleum, 1798, is an excellent example of how his work resonates with Mies van der Rohe's sensibilities. Mies transforms the monumental work into something that dissolves boundaries rather than reinforcing them and reimagines these spatial ideas in a way that merges

[2]   Rudolph Steiner, Bausteine zu einer Erkenntnis des Mysteriums von Golgatha, Dornach, 1996, GA 175, p. 44.

[3]   Rudolph Steiner, Das Verhältnis der verschiedenen naturwissenschaftlichen Gebiete zur Astronomie, Dornach, 1997, GA 323, pp. 119, 353.

[4]   Palden Jenkins, http://cura.free.fr/xx/20palden.html (last accessed March 30, 2025).

[5]   Alfred von Wolzogen, Aus Schinkel's Nachlaß. Reisetagebücher, Briefe und Aphorismen, vol. 2, Berlin, 1862, p. 211.

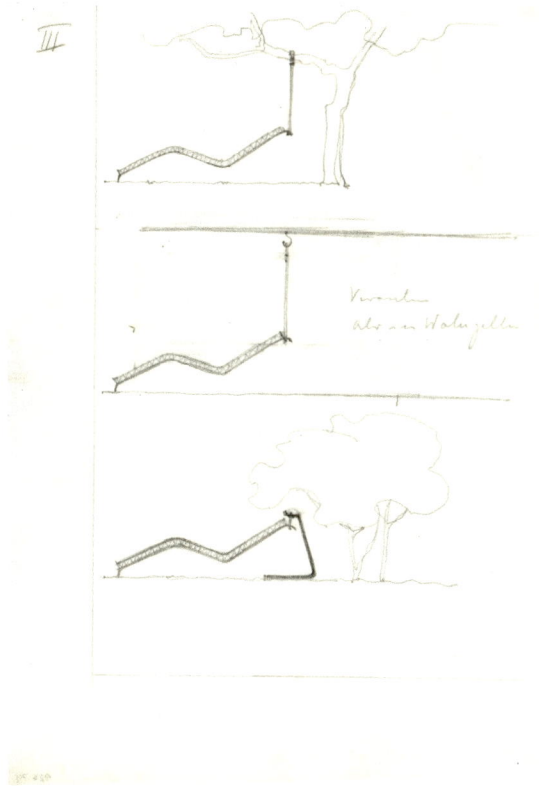

6 Ludwig Mies van der Rohe (March 27, 1886–August 17, 1969), design for a reclining chair, circa 1931, Museum of Modern Art, New York

the interior and exterior. The lack of ornamentation in Gilly's pillared hall and Mies van der Rohe's furniture should not be misinterpreted. No ornament is an ornament. With Mies, we can see that his ornament is in the grain of the wood or stone he uses, and on the surface of the tubular steel. Polished tubular steel, as used in his furniture designs such as the Barcelona chair or the F42E multifunctional lounge chair, captures and reflects its surroundings. These reflections create an ever-changing, subtle ornament that integrates the object into its spatial context, a new objectivity.

The aim of this book is to explore the process of how this Neue Sachlichkeit, or New Objectivity, came about, and what subjectivity or expressionism lay between the objectivity of the Arts and

Crafts movement of the 1900s and the emergence of the New Objectivity or, more popularly, the Bauhaus. It seeks to illuminate the development and cultural shifts that bridged these two approaches to design. Philosopher Hermann Graf von Keyserling (1880–1946) observed that objectivity in the good sense does not mean impersonal but rather the personal interest of the higher self, that is, the personal interest of the most deeply personal in the living human being, to whom consequently all the passion of self-discovery belongs.[6] He rejected all other objectivity because it would place dead things above life.

The early 20th century marked a critical juncture in German design, with Berlin emerging as the center of an innovative aesthetic movement that I call Berlin Deko. Spanning the years 1910 to 1930, this period embodies a remarkable synthesis of tradition and transformation, revealing the cultural tensions and aspirations of an era in flux. Far from being a mere prelude to modernism, Berlin Deko demands recognition as a phenomenon in its own right. It is a testament to interior design's ability to navigate between competing forces: past and present, local and global, harmony and upheaval. This is particularly evident in furniture, as the movable within the immovable. The tension between craft and innovation was further highlighted by the art critic Julius Meier-Graefe's (1867–1935) view that Kunsthandwerk (arts and crafts) represented a retreat from the progressive aims of fine art[7]—a critique that spoke directly to Berlin Deko's complex position between tradition and modernity.

The development of Berlin Deko took place against a backdrop of profound socio-political change in a decentralized Europe. It was in Munich that the Werkbund was founded in 1907. With the involvement of Karl Ernst Osthaus (1874–1921), the founder of Museum Folkwang in Hagen, the 1914 Werkbund Exhibition was held in Cologne.

6   Hermann Keyserling, Der Sinn der Persönlichkeit, in: Innendekoration, 1927, p. 82.
7   Julius Meier-Graefe, Entwicklungsgeschichte der modernen Kunst, vol. 2, Munich, 1966, p. 681.

7 Hermann Knackfuß (August 11, 1848–May 17, 1915), based on a design by Emperor Wilhelm II (January 27, 1857–June 4, 1941), Allegory "Peoples of Europe, safeguard your most sacred goods," lithograph, 1895/1904

It was also in Munich that artists such as Bruno Paul and Theodor Veil (1879–1965) were invited to participate in exhibitions in Paris and Brussels in 1910 (fig. 12). Paul set up an office in Berlin in 1905, where Mies joined him to work on furniture design. As in previous centuries, Berlin attracted creative people from abroad, but this time from even further afield. Oskar Kaufmann came from Hungary, John A. Campbell (1878–1948) from England, Karl Pullich (1884–1934) from the USA and Michael Rachlis (1884–1953) from Russia. While Europe grappled with imperial anxieties, such as Kaiser Wilhelm II's warnings against an "Asian threat," Berlin Deko designers embraced these very

"foreign" influences, incorporating Asian, Middle Eastern, and African motifs into their work. This cultural paradox manifested itself in domestic objects, such as a stove decorated with Buddhist imagery. A design that transformed symbols of fear into expressions of *Geborgenheit*, a deeply German notion of comfort and security.

Public figures such as Herwarth Walden (1878–1941), Harry Graf Kessler (1868–1937), Albert Einstein (1879–1955), and Walter Rathenau (1867–1922) embodied the spirit of innovation and cultural transformation that defined the city of Berlin at the time. Inspired by Henry David Thoreau's novel

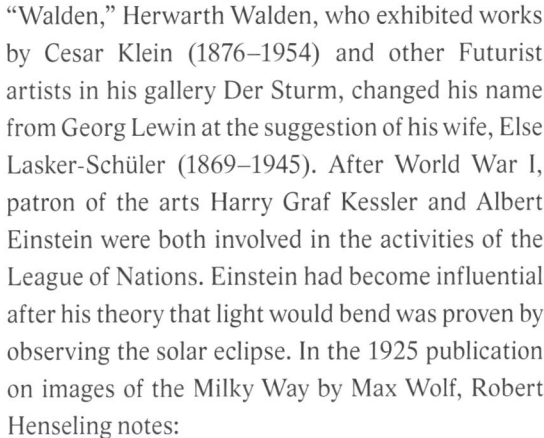

8 Unknown, tiled stove, manufactured by SOMAG, Meissen, circa 1920, Museum of Architecture, Wrocław

9 Detail of fig. 8

"Walden," Herwarth Walden, who exhibited works by Cesar Klein (1876–1954) and other Futurist artists in his gallery Der Sturm, changed his name from Georg Lewin at the suggestion of his wife, Else Lasker-Schüler (1869–1945). After World War I, patron of the arts Harry Graf Kessler and Albert Einstein were both involved in the activities of the League of Nations. Einstein had become influential after his theory that light would bend was proven by observing the solar eclipse. In the 1925 publication on images of the Milky Way by Max Wolf, Robert Henseling notes:

"But whoever is vividly aware of what the recent past has revealed about the nature of the Milky Way as the result of thousands of years of cognitive effort, whoever sees in it with the inner eye the multitudes of world clouds stratified into all the depths of the boundlessness of millions and millions of solar unities—the sight of the Milky Way may well become even more than the proclamation of beauty and mystery, namely the highest parable appearing in the sensual for the fact that harmony stands above all confused fate as the ultimate destiny."[8]

Despite these observations of unfathomable infinity, the reality of the earth needed to be digested. As Josephine Baker (1906–1975) rode through Berlin in a carriage drawn by an ostrich, the author Robert Musil (1880–1942), in his novel *The Man Without Qualities*, alluded to Walter Rathenau through the character of Paul Arnheim, who embodied the intellectual, cultural, and economic sophistication of the German elite. Rathenau himself was an industrialist, writer, and political visionary who championed ideas of international cooperation

---

8 Max Wolf, Die Milchstrasse und die kosmischen Nebel, Potsdam, 1925, p. 2.

10 Richard Böhland (1868–1935), watercolor after Walter Rathenau's dining room, Berlin–Grunewald, Moderne Bauformen, 1912

11 Winold Reiss (September 16, 1886–August 23, 1953), dining chair for the Alamac grill room, New York, 1923, Bernhard Goldenberg Fine Arts, LLC, New York

12 Theodor Veil (June 24, 1879–October 25, 1965), representative space for the 1910 Paris Salon d'Automne, Moderne Bauformen, 1910

13 Unknown, a German armoire, lacquered wood and gesso, dated 1926, Doris Leslie Blau, Ltd, New York

and modernization deeply rooted in the Enlightenment values of rationality and progress. Yet the inclusion of Arnheim's servant, Soliman—a young African boy—reveals the troubling hypocrisies that underpinned this supposedly enlightened cosmopolitanism.

Across the Atlantic in America, two Germans, the artist Winold Reiss (1886–1953) and the art historian Aby Warburg (1866–1929), took different approaches to cultural diversity. Both challenged cultural dominance through their work. Warburg's 1923 talk "A Lecture on Serpent Ritual" at the Bellevue Sanatorium in Kreuzlingen, Switzerland, explored his observations of Hopi rituals during his trip to the American Southwest in 1895. He used the Hopi snake ritual—a dance involving live snakes as intermediaries with the divine—to illustrate key ideas in his wider cultural and art historical research.

Also in 1923 Winold Reiss's designs for the Alamac Hotel in Manhattan[9] reflected a fascination with "the other" amid rapid industrialization. The German Black Forest is combined with the Congo. In the foyer, a large mouth allowed a view into the

dining room. This mythical energy parallels the symbolic power of Moloch in the Italian film *Cabiria* (1914), where the idol devours human sacrifices. Returning to Berlin, Fritz Lang (1890–1976) reinvented the motif in *Metropolis* (1927)—the consuming power of industry—as the industrial

---

9   Marilyn Satin Kushner, The Art of Winold Reiss. An Immigrant Modernist, New York, 2021, p. 223.

machine itself, a mechanical Moloch demanding the sacrifice of workers to sustain the city. This theme finds a linguistic counterpart in Prague, where Karel Čapek (1890–1938) introduced the word "robot" in his 1920 play *R.U.R.* (Rossum's Universal Robots). Derived from the Czech word *robota* (forced labour), the term crystallized anxieties about mechanization and dehumanization, reflecting the same fears that Lang's Moloch machine visualized on screen.

Berlin, especially during the Weimar period, can be seen as a juggernaut in its own right. The city's relentless pace and cultural vibrancy demanded constant labor and sacrifice, embodying the seductive yet devouring nature of modernity. Berlin was a space of both mythic possibility and existential

cost. If this dramaturgy had been translated into form, the resulting number of pieces of furniture would have remained rare.

The art historical reception of these designs matured in the 1990s with significant exhibitions and scholarly works reshaping our understanding of this aesthetic. In his article "Bruno Paul and the Other Modernism," in a 1992 Munich exhibition catalog, Hans Ottomeier began, "While our ideas about the beginning of modernism in the 20th century seem to follow a straight line from Jugendstil to the Werkbund, the Bauhaus, and

the accepted maxims and solutions of industrial design, Bruno Paul's oeuvre confronts us with an entirely different reality and set of phenomena."[10] The ideology of a pure form, which consequently had to be politically correct, was coming to an end. Catarina Berents's 1994 dissertation on Art Deco in Germany then focused exclusively on modern ornament.[11] This helped to identify German works and further distinguish them from Austrians such as Dagobert Peche, whose work was celebrated in a retrospective at the Museum für angewandte Kunst in Vienna in 1998.[12]

The first exhibition, titled *Berlin Deko*, took place in 2015 at the Brian Kish Gallery in New York, where I showed parts of my collection for the first time.

In Berlin in 2016, Tobias Hoffmann, director of the Bröhan-Museum, opened an exhibition called *Germany vs. France, the Battle for Style 1900–1930.*

---

[10] Alfred Ziffer, Bruno Paul. Deutsche Raumkunst und Architektur zwischen Jugendstil und Moderne, Munich, 1992, p. 105.

[11] Catharina Berents, Art Déco in Deutschland. Das moderne Ornament, Frankfurt am Main, 1997.

[12] Peter Noever, Die Überwindung der Utilität. Dagobert Peche und die Wiener Werkstätte, Ostfildern, 1998.

14   Berlin Deko exhibition, installation view,
Brian Kish Gallery, New York, 2015

15   Fernando Santangelo,
Berlin Deko tea room,
New York, 2016

In the catalog he quoted Bruno Paul's words for the 1927 Biennale in Monza, Italy, who said: "The form of present and future things will flow together in a world style, but will have very different expressions. It will grow out of different conditions in the south than in the north, and local inclinations and differences in temperament will forcibly give rise to a wealth of divergent solutions." Hoffmann elaborated on how Walter Gropius had succeeded Paul in organizing the Werkbund's representation at the Salon des Artistes Décorateurs in Paris in 1930. Gropius seized this opportunity to present "his Bauhaus" to the French public,[13] an initiative that significantly shaped the global perception of German design.

The exposure of Berlin Deko furniture reached a preliminary high point with the exhibition at Schloß Wernigerode in 2019.[14] Held in the castle's historic rooms, renovated in the Art Déco style during 1919/20, this exhibition showcased furniture by Leo Nachtlicht for the first time in a German museum. What had previously been perceived as another modernism became a poetic[15] modernism, as Don Freeman documented for *The World of Interiors*[16] magazine. The selection of works illustrated is by no means exhaustive. It is my intention, however, to introduce the reader to important works of the period. The order is not chronological, but through the lens of discovery—both personal and scholarly.

[13]   Tobias Hoffmann, Deutschland gegen Frankreich – Der Kampf um den Stil 1900–1930, Cologne, 2016, p. 204.

[14]   Christian Juranek, Art Déco: Kunst des Historismus? (Edition Schloß Wernigerode, vol. 22), Wettin-Löbejün, 2019.

[15]   Norbert Hanenberg, lecture: Eduard Pfeiffer. Ein Dichter unter den Architekten, Germanisches Nationalmuseum, Nuremberg, 2022.

[16]   Tomothy Brittain-Catlin, Double Deutsch, in: The World of Interiors, London, May 2019, pp. 182–189.

PHOTO GALLERY

principal photography by

Don Freeman

text by Markus Winter

Setup for Berlin Deko photo shoot, Raddestorf, Germany, 2016

The conical-shaped corpus is modeled on Egyptian furniture, which was introduced to Germany around 1800. The hexagonal cartouches depict floral and geometric motifs from northern Europe. This combination of influences demonstrates the melding of two distinct cultural traditions.

17 Karl Pullich (1884–1934) (?), commode, carved and veneered birch, circa 1917, private collection

18 John A. Campbell, study for a bedroom in a country house, Innendekoration, 1909

GEORG SCHOETTLE
KÖNIGLICHE HOFMÖBELFABRIK · STVTTGART.

Karl Pullich was born in New York. In 1905, he joined his brother Otto Pullich and John Archibald (Ino A.) Campbell (May 3, 1878–August 19, 1948) in the company Campbell & Pullich in Berlin. After spending time in London, New York, and Munich, Karl began working for Georg Schoettle in Stuttgart in 1912.

19 Karl Pullich, advertisement for furniture maker Georg Schoettle, Dekorative Kunst, 1920

Compared to the chair in Hugo Gorge's interior, this so-called Chinoiserie version could be considered relatively conservative. It may have been part of an aristocratic setting at Schloß Berchtesgaden.

20 Kunsthaus L. Bernheimer (?), armchair, gilt and lacquered wood, circa 1922, private collection

21 Hugo Gorge, (January 31, 1883–December 25, 1934) veranda, Innendekoration 1921

22 Bruno Paul (January 19, 1874–August 17, 1968), armchair, carved mahogany, manufactured by Deutsche Werkstätten Dresden-Hellerau, 1935, private collection

23 Bruno Paul, interior, Deutsche Werkstätten AG, Dresden-Hellerau, 1935, Brochure

Paul used this armrest shape as early as 1928.[1] Here he incorporates a Murano chandelier by Vittorio Zecchin into his furnishings.

---

[1] Bruckmann, Dekorative Kunst, Munich, 1929, p. 161.

24   Leo Nachtlicht (August 12, 1872–September 22, 1942),
side table, wood lacquered in RAL 1019 gray beige, glass top,
circa 1922, private collection

This table may have been part of a commission
together with the vanity table in fig. 97. Here
Nachtlicht frames the glass top with a large grooved
edge profile. The legs are again very abstract, like
saber legs in neoclassical furniture.

25   Unknown, dining chair, carved and veneered zebrano, aluminum, glass, Rhineland, circa 1928, private collection

Originally part of a dining room with sideboard fig. 66. The curule seat has been elongated and transformed into a New Objectivity form.

26　Oskar Kaufmann (February 2, 1873–September 8, 1956), dining chair for Villa Leo Lewin in Breslau, carved rosewood, 1917, private collection

27 Oskar Kaufmann, dining chair for Villa Leo Lewin in Breslau, carved rosewood, 1917, Der Architekt Oskar Kaufmann, 1928

The chair combines several sources: Frederick the Great Rococo forms, especially the design of the feet, inspired by the furniture designs of Johann Michael Hoppenhaupt the Elder, 18th century; then again, the shape of the back echoes English Baroque designs. The carvings themselves are of exotic (non-European) flowers: Egyptian, agave or birds of paradise, for example. A fruit skin could be suggested by the fillet that runs down the left and right sides of the chair's front legs. These exotic flowers are similar to those used by Cesar Klein in his stained glass and mosaic works. On the other hand, there are references to the spirituality of Munich Art Nouveau, such as Bernhard Pankok. It is possible that this chair is the first example of an Expressionist Rococo style. Designers will later look to Kaufman's exoticizing style for direction.

28 Johann Michael Hoppenhaupt the elder, (1709–after 1755), drawing for a chest of drawers, Berlin, circa 1740

29   Detail of fig. 30

30 Karl Pullich (1884–1934) (?), longcase clock, carved and veneered oak, southwestern Germany, dated 1914, private collection

31 Eduard Pfeiffer (March 4, 1889–October 21, 1929), interior for a private home in Cologne, Deutsche Kunst und Dekoration, 1920

CAMPBELL
& PVLLICH:

ARCHITEKTEN :

BERLIN :

32 Campbell & Pullich, advertisement, Deutsche Kunst und Dekoration, 1908

34   Emil Fahrenkamp,
(November 8, 1885–May 24, 1966),
living room in the Filius house,
Innendekoration, 1921

33   Unknown, demilune cabinet, black lacquer and gilt,
Rhineland, circa 1922, private collection

As with armoire fig. 13, cabinets fig. 75 and fig. 140, a central lesena separates the left and right doors, the male and female sides. The top edge has no moldings. The closed doors rest on the body and do not close flush. Both stylistic features are very indicative of the New Objectivity. There is cherry veneer under the black French polish and inlays under the stucco decoration. It is most likely, however, that the furniture was given a different finish in the 1920s at the latest. The ornamentation and the way it is placed on the panels can be compared to the work of Emil Fahrenkamp.

35   Detail of fig. 38

36   Detail of fig. 38

37   Fritz August Breuhaus, sideboard for a Cologne dining room, Innendekoration, 1921

38   Fritz August Breuhaus (February 9, 1883–December 2, 1960) (?), floor lamp, carved walnut, later shade, Rhineland, circa 1920, private collection

It is worth noting the stylized figure of a reader on the rustic plinth. This type of Renaissance bust can also be found on other furniture, such as a sideboard by Breuhaus.

29

39 Lajos Kozma (June 8, 1884–November 26, 1948), side chair, carved and veneered walnut, circa 1925, private collection

40 Lajos Kozma, "The Mirror" study, dated 1918, Innendekoration, 1922

41 Bruno Paul (January 19, 1874–August 17, 1968),
table for the salon of the Reichsbahn director of Altona,
Macassar ebony carved and veneered,
1909, private collection

42 Ernst Böhm (6 March 1890–2 September 1963),
vase/lamp base, large double gourd, in the German section
at the international exhibition in Monza, 1927,
porcelain, Staatliche Porzellan-Manufaktur Berlin, 1926,
Bröhan-Museum, Berlin, inv. no. 91–009,
Deutsche Kunst und Dekoration, 1927

43 | 44   Heinrich Vogeler
(December 12, 1872–June 14, 1942),
bench, stained and carved oak, manufactured
by Worpsweder Werkstätten, circa 1905–1910,
Bröhan-Museum, Berlin, inv. no. 13-077b

45 Paul Thiersch (May 2, 1879–November 15, 1928),
sideboard buffet, American walnut, manufactured by
cabinetmaker Otto Jüdersleben, Berlin, 1912,
Bröhan-Museum, Berlin. inv. no. 97–004

46 Paul Thiersch, dining room at Landhaus Syla, Neumark,
Deutsche Kunst und Dekoration, 1914

Like architecture within architecture, the
monumental dimensions of Thiersch's sideboards,
inspired by Platonic forms and the golden ratio,[2]
seem to dominate the spaces in which they were
placed.

---

[2] Fabian Reifferscheidt, in: Tobias Hoffmann, Deutschland
     gegen Frankreich. Der Kampf um den Stil 1900–1930,
     Cologne, 2016, p. 183.

47 Paul Thiersch, chair, American walnut, manufactured
by cabinetmaker Otto Jüdersleben, Berlin, 1912,
Bröhan-Museum, Berlin. inv. no. 97–004b.1

48 | 49 Franz Haegele (1886–1969), chandelier,
nickel-plated brass, manufactured by Schwintzer & Gräf,
circa 1925, Bröhan-Museum, Berlin, inv. no. 83–005

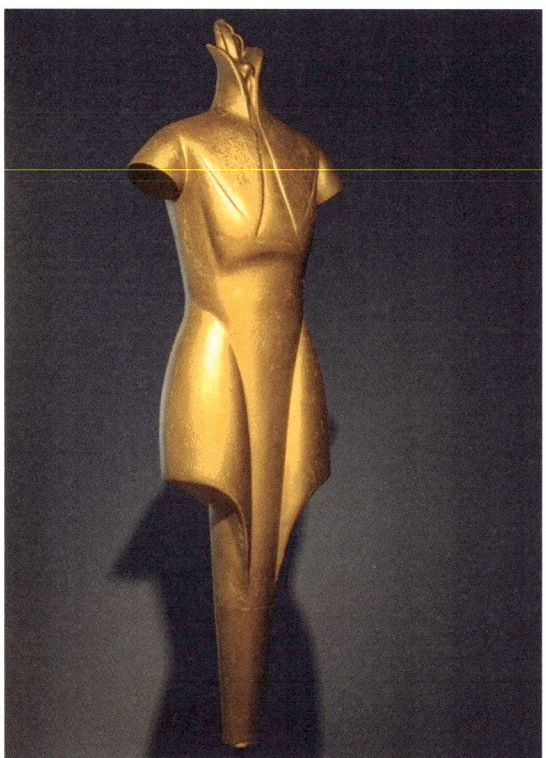

50 Rudolf Belling (August 26, 1886–June 9, 1972),
mannequin, manufactured by Erdmannsdorfer Büstenfabrik
A-G. Berlin, 1923, papier-mâché,
Bröhan-Museum, Berlin, inv. no. 15–011

The rose motif may have resulted from the collaboration with Joseph Wackerle (May 15, 1880–March 20, 1959). The diagonal pattern implies Italian and French marquetry but also much older sources such as mummy dressings. Kaufmann would use this diagonal pattern at the same time as Troost, transforming it into more free compositions by the 1920s.

51 Paul Ludwig Troost (August 17, 1878–January 21, 1934), cabinet, rosewood veneered and inlaid with various woods, manufactured by Vereinigte Werkstätten für Kunst im Handwerk, Munich, circa 1910, private collection

53 Mummy, Egypt, between 30 BCE and 395 CE, Detroit Institute of Arts

52 Oskar Kaufmann (February 2, 1873–September 8, 1956), lady's room in his own apartment, Deutsche Kunst und Dekoration, 1911

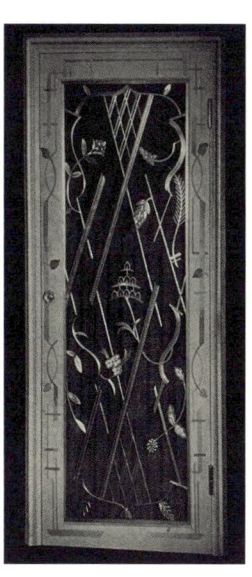

54 Oskar Kaufmann, radiator casing for Die Komödie theater, Berlin, 1924

Few 20th-century furniture designs embody the union of symbol and ritual like this dressing mirror. Here it becomes clear: Berlin Deko furniture lives between two mythic extremes. Either it answers, like the Epic of Gilgamesh, to the ever-present adventure for daily survival, or it anticipates, like the ancient Egyptians, the provisions necessary for a beatific afterlife.

55 | 56 Emil Fahrenkamp (November 8, 1885–May 24, 1966), vanity for a private commission together with table fig. 129, lacquered wood, circa 1920, private collection

57   Hugo Gorge (January 31, 1883–December 25, 1934), armchair, maple, manufactured by Kunst und Wohnung R. Lorenz GmbH, Vienna, circa 1923

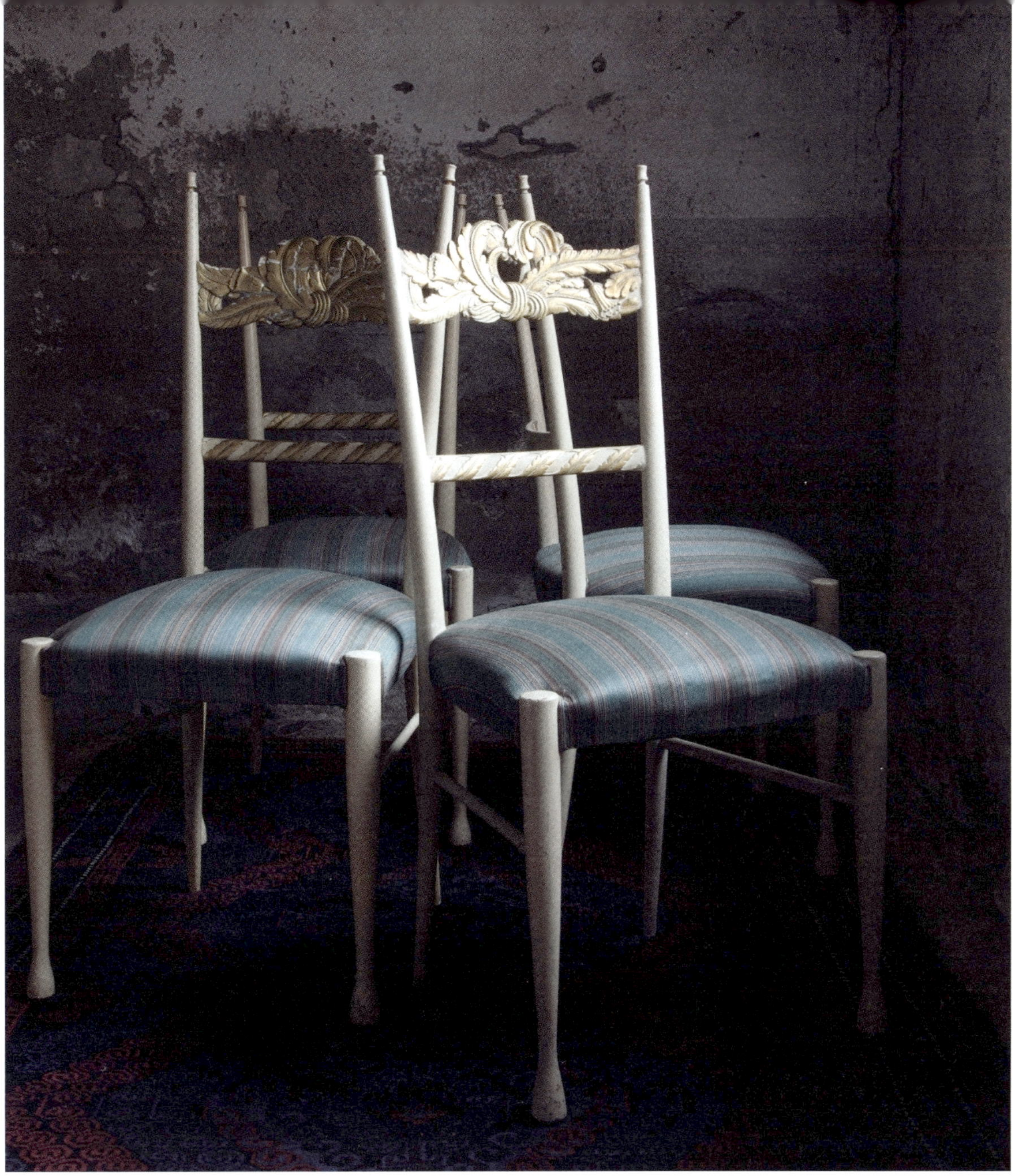

58   Paolo Buffa (1903–1970) and Giovanni Gariboldi
(1908–1971), set of chairs, lacquered walnut and gold leaf,
manufactured by Serafino Arrighi, Cantù,
1950, private collection

The influence of German-speaking architects such
as the Viennese Hugo Gorge and Rudolf Alexander
Schröder from Bremen (January 26, 1878–August
22, 1962) on post-war Italian designers is difficult to
overestimate.[3]

59   Hugo Gorge, memorial room in the exhibition of the
Austrian Werkbund, Innendekoration, 1937

[3]   Deutsche Kunst und Dekoration, 1911, p. 108.

60   Bruno Paul (January 19, 1874–August 17, 1968),
display cabinet, mahogany carved and veneered,
probably manufactured by Zoo-Werkstätten,
Berlin, circa 1923,
sculpture by Alexander Knych on a pedestal by
Charles Spindler (March 11, 1865–March 3, 1938),
private collection

61 Bruno Paul (January 19, 1874–August 17, 1968), display cabinet detail of fig. 60

The base cabinet employs the multiply repeated curvature of a Braunschweig chest of drawers, at the same time creating a vitrine top which remains in Paul's habitual classical manner.

62 Bruno Paul, dining room for the house of Mia and Carl Bergman, *Deutsche Kunst und Dekoration*, 1930

63 John Archibald (Ino A.) Campbell
(May 3, 1878–August 19, 1948),
dining chair for Ludwig Hupfeld,
Leipzig, carved walnut, manufactured
by Pössenbacher Werkstätten,
Munich, 1910, private collection

64 Carl Müller, living room,
Innendekoration, 1924

German Reform architecture integrated the English
forms brought by Campbell into its designs.

65 Ino A. Campbell, dining room for Ludwig Hupfeld,
Leipzig, Innendekoration, 1912

66 Unknown, sideboard, carved and veneered zebrano, aluminum, glass, Rhineland, circa 1928, originally part of a dining room with chair (fig. 25), private collection

Like the cabinet in a watercolor by Bernhard Pfau, both pieces share the metal central lesena, but the difference here is that the body of the furniture is half wrapped in an undulating ribbon, creating space for additional shelves and drawers.

67 Bernhard Pfau (June 1, 1902–July 30, 1989), watercolor for Atelier Emil Fahrenkamp, Moderne Bauformen, 1928

68 Hermann Straub, sideboard, zebrano with intarsia, produced by B. Disselmann & Sohn, Cologne, Moderne Bauformen, 1929

69   After Lajos Kozma (June 8, 1884–November 26, 1948),
armoire, painted wood, Germany,
circa 1926, private collection

70   Lajos Kozma, design for a painted armoire, dated 1922,
Farbige Wohnräume der Neuzeit, 1926

71 Eduard Pffeiffer (March 4, 1889–October 21, 1929),
armchair, carved walnut, manufactured by Pössenbacher Werkstätten, Munich,
circa 1911, private collection

72   Detail of fig. 71

74   Eduard Pfeiffer, armchair in the yellow salon at hotel Atlantic, Deutsche Kunst und Dekoration, 1912, Germanisches Nationalmuseum, Nuremberg

Whereas the front legs of the armchairs exhibit Asian influences, the backrest incorporates elements of the Arts and Crafts movement, and the armrests are inspired by 17th-century Venetian design.[4]

This eclectic combination reflects Pfeiffer's approach to blending different stylistic references while maintaining a sense of historical ambiguity.

73   Detail of fig. 71

4   See: Sotheby's, The Collection of Count and Countess Volpi di Misurata. Palazzo Volpi Unveiled. Paris, February 28, 2024, lot 58.

75   Eduard Pfeiffer (March 4, 1889–October 21, 1929),
two-part cabinet, carved oak, possibly manufactured
by Pössenbacher Werkstätten, Munich,
circa 1920, private collection

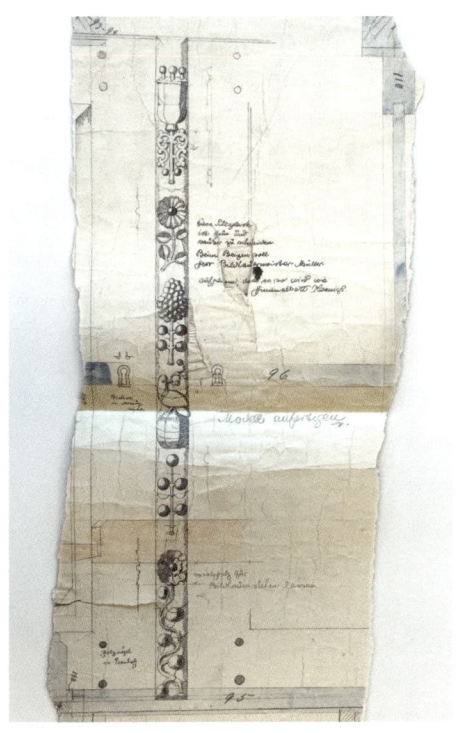

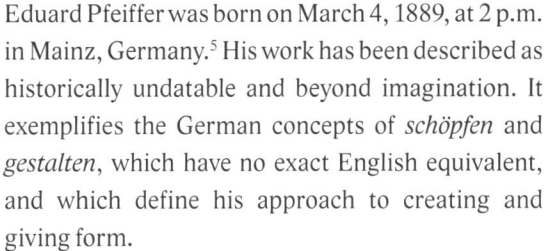

76 Eduard Pfeiffer, drawing for a cabinet, circa 1912,
Germanisches Nationalmuseum, Nuremberg

77 Detail of fig. 75

Eduard Pfeiffer was born on March 4, 1889, at 2 p.m. in Mainz, Germany.[5] His work has been described as historically undatable and beyond imagination. It exemplifies the German concepts of *schöpfen* and *gestalten*, which have no exact English equivalent, and which define his approach to creating and giving form.

Although Eduard Pfeiffer's cabinet refers to an un-identifiable period, it integrates stylistic elements from different regions and epochs. The hanging and ornate apron is a feature of Dutch furniture. In Pfeiffer's case, however, this design element is taken to an exaggerated level, elevating the otherwise classical element to a more contemporary, avant-garde statement. The cartouche under the cornice, deliberately left uncarved and devoid of any heraldic emblem, implies an imagined leadership rather than an inherited or historically established authority.

78 Eduard Pfeiffer, living room and library
for the Werkbund Exhibition in Cologne,
Deutsche Kunst und Dekoration, 1914

---

5 Friendly note by Norbert Hanenberg.

79 Fritz August Breuhaus (February 9, 1883–December 2, 1960) (?),
library table, carved oak, veneered and inlayed table top,
circa 1914, private collection

80 Fritz August Breuhaus, table lamp, carved mahogany, manufactured by Mikado-Werkstätten A.-G. Bonn, circa 1923, private collection

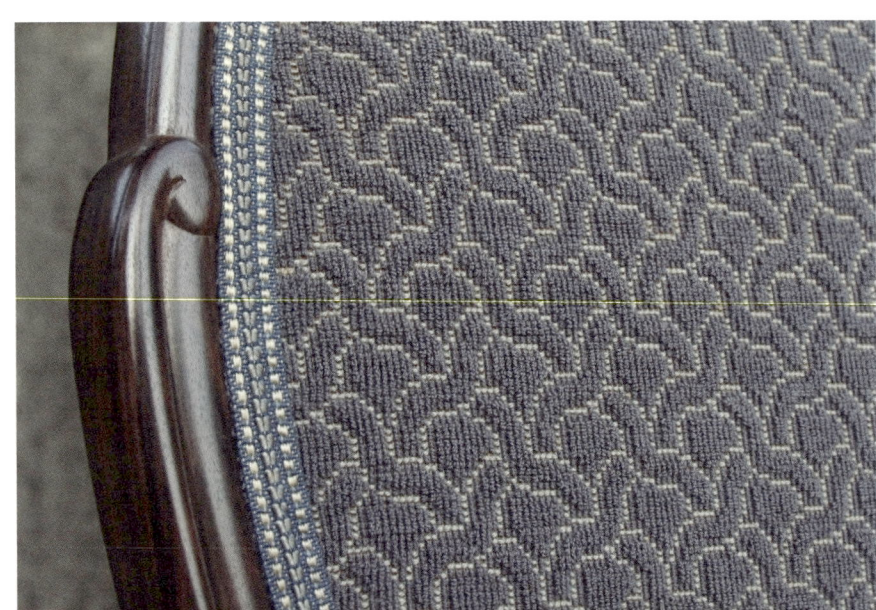

81 | 82   Bruno Paul (January 19, 1874–August 17, 1968),
dining chair and footrest for the salon of the Reichsbahn director of Altona,
Macassar ebony, original fabric, 1909, private collection

83   Emil Fahrenkamp (November 8, 1885–May 24, 1966), table for the hotel Vier Jahreszeiten in Hamburg, solid walnut and marble top, circa 1926, private collection

84   Bernhard Hoetger (November 8, 1885–May 24, 1966), Tree of Life on the façade of the Atlantis building, Bremen, 1930/31, Archive Böttcherstraße

85   Emil Fahrenkamp, tea room with gallery for the hotel Vier Jahreszeiten, Hamburg, Innendekoration, 1926

Designed for the interior of the hotel Vier Jahreszeiten, this table by Emil Fahrenkamp exhibits a composition similar to the basic elements Bernhard Hoetger utilized in his project in Bremen, the Atlantis building, where he thought to visualize esoteric themes.

86   Oskar Kaufmann (February 2, 1873–September 8, 1956),
sconce for Leo Lewin, Breslau, gilt wood and glass,
1917, private collection

87   Detail of fig. 86

89   Oskar Kaufmann, dining room
for Leo Lewin, Breslau, 1917

88   Carl August Mencke, probably after a design by Karl
Friedrich Schinkel (March 13, 1781–October 9 1841),
sconce, gilded wood, cast iron, pewter,
Berlin, circa 1820, Frank C. Möller Fine Arts, Hamburg

This light-bearer with a patinated surface suggests
an object of historical significance. This approach
follows the method of Carl Friedrich Schinkel, who
used classical references to create designs that evoke
the past. The patina applied to Kaufmann's sconces
reinforces the impression of an artifact, linking the
present with antiquity.

90 Oskar Kaufmann (February 2, 1873–September 8, 1956), buffet cabinets for Leo Lewin, Breslau, veneered rosewood, marble top, interior mahogany with intarsia after Max Slevogt, Berlin, 1917, private collection

91 Oskar Kaufmann (February 2, 1873–September 8, 1956),
buffet cabinets for Leo Lewin, Breslau, veneered rosewood,
marble top, interior mahogany with intarsia after
Max Slevogt, Berlin, 1917, private collection

92 Richard Teschner (1879–1948), commode in the lady's
bedroom of Dr. Josef Kranz, Vienna, Dekorative Kunst, 1917

Both Kaufmann and Teschner explored Baroque
and Mannerist influences, particularly the
Bohemian Baroque tradition, to which Kaufmann
explicitly referred. Their furniture shares the architectural dynamism of undulating, sculptural
facades. Kaufmann's work, in particular, echoes the
layout of Michelangelo's staircase in the Biblioteca
Medicea Laurenziana in Florence, where the central
sweeping form is flanked by smaller, structured
elements, mirroring the rhythm of these cabinets.

The marquetry is in the tradition of David Rontgen
(1743–1807), yet an independent development can
be discerned. The interplay of content and form is of
exemplary quality.

93   Ernst Nast (?), intarsia "Gesang" (song) after
Max Slevogt, Berlin, private collection

94   Ernst Nast (?), intarsia "Weib" (woman) after
Max Slevogt, Berlin, missing

96   Ernst Nast (?), intarsia "Wein" (wine) after
Max Slevogt, Berlin, private collection

95   Workshop of David Roentgen
(August 11, 1743–February 12, 1807), marquetry panel
of a longcase clock after a design by Thomas Chippendale
1718–1779, signed Reusch, Neuwied, circa 1774,
The Metropolitan Museum of Art, New York

97　Franz Xaver Unterseher (January 25, 1888–April 12, 1954),
tabernacle mirror, carved and painted wood, circa 1925.
Museum Schloß Wernigerode

Leo Nachtlicht (August 12, 1872–September 22, 1942),
vanity table, wood lacquered in RAL 1019 gray beige,
circa 1922, private collection, might have been part
of a commission together with the side table fig. 24

98 Franz Xaver Unterseher, tabernacle frame,
Deutsche Illustrierte Rundschau, 1927

99 Leo Nachtlicht, boudoir in the house of Dr. Schwalbe,
Innendekoration, 1922

The concept of the tabernacle mirror alludes
to the idea that one must open doors to see
one's true self. The mirror's alternative use
as a picture of Mary may also point to the
spiritual aspects of this ritual.

100   view of fig. 97

102   Karl Leuth, template, from *Wand- und Deckendekoration*,
Leipzig, 1928

103   Theodor Veil (June 24, 1879–October 25, 1965),
chair, oak, mother-of-pearl, rush, circa 1910,
painting by Joshua Abelow, private collection

The backrest of this chair is formed with vertical
columns, while in the drawing the backrest braces
are oriented horizontally.

101   After Karl Leuth, dollhouse cabinet, lacquered
wood, circa 1928, private collection

104   Theodor Veil & Gerhard Herms, design for
a ladies salon, Munich, Moderne Bauformen, 1912

105 Unknown, fragment, carved walnut,
circa 1919, private collection

106 Otto Prutscher (April 7, 1880–February 15, 1949) (?),
secretary, cherry wood and various intarsia woods,
circa 1924, private collection,
the top section replaced the original missing one

107
108
109
110
Details of fig. 106

The concept for this Biedermeier desk can be found in David and Friedrich Gilly's 18th-century designs for Japanese and Chinese pavilions above grottoes in the parks of Paretz and Freienwalde. Combining temple and grotto, earthly and celestial beings come together here. The grotto motif of the interior also reflects an exploration of the inner self. Meanwhile, the inlaid marquetry of an Asian temple on the case reflects the theme of serving spirituality. Architectural vision and furniture design merge to create an intimate space for contemplation.

Each side of the keys is marked with a different rune-like motif.

111   Otto Prutscher (7 April 1880–15 February 1949) (?),
room for a lady, Dekorative Kunst, 1925

112   Martin Friedrich Rabe (1765–1856) (?),
watercolor drawing for the grotto hill with the
Japanese pavilion at Paretz, between 1797 and 1811, SPSG

113 | 114 Ernst Haiger
(June 10, 1874–March 15, 1952),
commode, lacquered wood,
brass, marmor thessalicum top,
manufactured by Vereinigte
Werkstätten für Kunst im Handwerk,
circa 1912, private collection

The tapered legs reflect English design traditions, while the brass hardware is inspired by ancient Greek and Roman handles. The top is made of verde antico, a symbolic Thessalian marble used in Byzantine architecture, including the Hagia Sophia.

115 Markus Winter, living room with a sculpture
by Alexej Koschkarow, New York, 2017

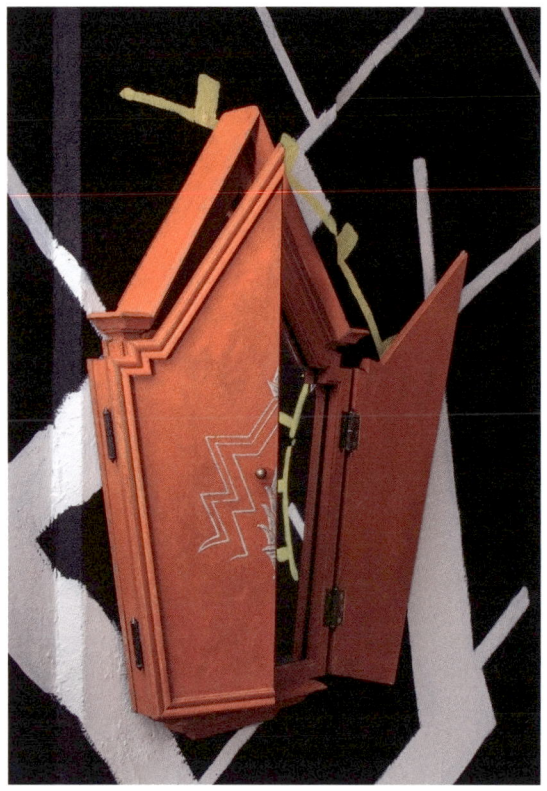

116 | 117 Unknown, tabernacle mirror, gessoed and lacquered wood, Rhineland, circa 1922, private collection

118 Runge & Scotland, drawing, Museum "Vätererbe" Bremen, Moderne Bauformen, 1928

The design of this tabernacle mirror combines the traditional northern German form of a Bückeburg wedding cabinet with the expressive ornamentation and color of the 1920s. Like the mirror in fig. 97, this piece invites the viewer to study his or her own metamorphosis.

119 | 120   Unknown, chandelier, carved and lacquered
wood, Budapest, circa 1920, private collection

121   Werry Roth (1885–1958), large hall in the clubhouse of
the Berlin Ice Skating Club, Moderne Bauformen, 1922

The central relief depicts a mature woman holding a bowl, reclining in a landscape of Mediterranean architecture and nature, while a separate goblet rests on a plate nearby. Design elements also found in the works of Oskar Kaufmann and Bruno Schneidereit are the pedestals to the left and right of the foot section.

Once owned by the actress Ute Willing in Berlin in the 1980s, this island-like stage can serve for different Hellenistic or Nordic mythological interpretations. The interplay of fertility, sensuality, and transience, captured in a veristic nude, makes this work a significant contribution to the interior design of New Objectivity and Magic Realism. But ultimately, with its children, sleep, and gentle death, the bed is the place where night transpires.

122   Unknown, bed, carved and lacquered wood,
Berlin, circa 1922, private collection

123　Detail of fig. 122

124　Bruno Schneidereit (*July 12, 1880),
bedroom of an actress, Berlin, Moderne Bauformen, 1923

Like Poelzig to his illuminated columns for the Großes Schauspielhaus, Kaufmann added indirect lighting to the center of the pendant. The stacked goblets had already appeared in Schinkel's designs, but here they were given a decisive twist. The

125   Oskar Kaufmann (February 2, 1873–September 8, 1956), ten-branch chandelier for Villa Leo Lewin, Breslau, silvered copper, manufactured by Hermann Noack, Berlin, 1917, private collection

connection between the central lotus cups and the individual light sources—also shaped as smaller lotus cups—is formed by an unadorned wave that serves as a channel for the electric current, an embodiment of the flow of energy as a visible frequency within the design.

126 Dagobert Peche (April 3, 1887–April 16, 1923),
pendant, brass, produced by Wiener Werkstätte,
Deutsche Kunst und Dekoration, 1921

127 Hans Poelzig (April 30, 1869–June 14, 1936),
Großes Schauspielhaus, Berlin, 1919

128 Karl Friedrich Schinkel (March 13, 1781–October 9, 1841),
Prinz-Albrecht-Palais, Berlin, 1831

129   Emil Fahrenkamp (November 8, 1885–May 24, 1966),
side table for a private commission together with
vanity fig. 56 and an armoire similar to fig. 132,
lacquered wood, circa 1921, private collection

130   Vittorio Zecchin (May 21, 1878–April 15, 1947),
pedestal, carved and silvered ash, Trieste,
circa 1923, private collection

131   Vittorio Zecchin, dining room at the international
exhibition in Monza, 1923

132   Emil Fahrenkamp (November 8, 1885–May 24, 1966),
armoire in a children's bedroom for the Schwickering house,
Dülmen, Innendekoration, 1923

The sculptor Artur Helbig was a student of Bruno Paul's at the Kunstgewerbemuseum in Berlin. Anton Jaumann wrote about Artur Helbig and his light fixtures in *Deutsche Kunst und Dekoration*:

"One must not assume that this youth groans heavily under the burden of tradition. They play ball with the centuries, with styles, with convictions. They learn—without reverence. They fight—without believing. They are bold—out of indifference. [...] The Indian, the Biedermeier, the Expressionist, who wants to define miscegenation? [...] The desirable fullness, the volume is achieved through the richness of craftsmanship, which manifests itself in a variety of ways. [...] The unified spirit of craftsmanship holds everything together. [...] The pieced-together unity is an attraction, like the clumsy daintiness and the borrowed naivety mixed with cabaret spirit."[6]

---

[6] Anton Jauman, in: Deutsche Kunst und Dekoration, 1923, p. 349.

133 | 134   Artur Helbig (?), wall sconces, cast brass, circa 1923, private collection

The glass shades are of a later date. They replaced what was most likely made of pleated paper. As the shades rest only on the head, the hands are free to carry and direct an imaginary energy.

135 | 136 Rudolf Kraus, vanity table and mirror,
walnut carved and veneered, marble,
Vienna, circa 1922, private collection

137 Rudolf Kraus, dressing mirror,
Moderne Bauformen, 1922

138   Still from the movie *Metropolis*, 1927

139   Unknown, candlesticks, turned Karelian birch, circa 1924, private collection

The birch tree embodies the symbolic qualities of light and renewal. Unlike the electrified light sources in *Metropolis* (1927), these objects retain the organic and traditional function of candlelight. Their geometric precision and layering suggest an interplay between nature and technology.

140 | 141 Lajos Kozma (June 8, 1884–November 26, 1948), walnut carved and veneered, manufactured by Kozma's Budapest workshop, circa 1912, private collection

Both Pfeiffer and Campbell used the shape of the double arch in their designs, looking back at earlier English furniture. Kozma, in contrast, combines the Hungarian folkloristic aspect and adds a carved relief with high plasticity.

142 | 143   Bruno Paul
(January 19, 1874–August 17, 1968),
New York sideboard, stained birch carved
and veneered, silvered brass fittings,
Berlin Zoo-Werkstätten #51961,
1928, private collection

Paul Huwald, candle sconces, chased brass, Kiel,
circa 1906, private collection

Here, in this seemingly modernist furniture,
one can also recognize a Chinese altar table
on top of an Egyptian coffin-like cube.

144   Kunst und Wohnung, Rudolf Lorenz (?),
sideboard, walnut carved and veneered, intarsia
with ash, maple, and other woods, Vienna,
circa 1926, private collection

145 Oskar Strnad (26 October 1879–3 September 1935), lounge chair, mahogany, circa 1920, private collection

146   Oskar Strnad, reception room,
Deutsche Kunst und Dekoration, 1917

Strnad used this lounge chair in several variations.
This design is closer to the New Objectivity or Neues
Wiener Wohnen movement pioneered by Strnad
and Josef Frank (July 15, 1885–January 8, 1967).
Arms with outscrolled terminals, as on this chair,
can also be found in the work of William Kent.[7]

147   Oskar Strnad, presentation space for painting,
sculpture, etc. in the *Austrian House* at the Werkbund
Exhibition, Cologne, 1914

---

7   Christie's, sale 15785, New York 2017, lot 106.

148 Fritz August Breuhaus
(February 9, 1883–December 2, 1960),
library cabinet, carved and veneered walnut,
veneered amboyna, partly ebonized,
manufactured by Valentin Witt,
Munich and Cologne,
circa 1914, private collection

Architectural elements, as known from the Weser Renaissance, were combined here with Pompeian-style handles and folkloristic floral motifs under an early Baroque cornice. The floral carving motifs here are still naturalistic in their elaboration. Similar motifs were later used in a much more stylized manner. Rearing horses with raised tails as Westphalian steeds flank two arches reminiscent of a cabinet by Charles Guillaume Diehls. If one interprets this as a double portal flanked by pillars, then the oversized handles below could serve as ladder rungs for access to another sphere.

150 Jean Brandely, cabinet, Paris, 1867, The Metropolitan Museum of Art, New York, inv. no. 1989.197

151 Fritz August Breuhaus (February 9, 1883–December 2, 1960), library, Innendekoration, 1914

152 Johann Hundertossen († 1606), entrance portal, Bevern Castle, 1603–1612

153   Detail of four-door sideboard in fig. 15

154   Fritz August Breuhaus
(February 9, 1883–December 2, 1960) (?),
two sideboards, Brazilian rosewood carved
and veneered, the sculptures after Lotte Pritzel
(January 30, 1887–February 17, 1952),
western Germany, circa 1926, private collection

The dancing figures seem to capture the essence of expressive dance, particularly the choreography of Mary Wigman (1886–1973), who sought to make visible the inner experience of the human body. Fritz August Breuhaus, who had worked with Pritzel's dolls before World War I, designed the new home for Alexander Koch in 1925. Here Pritzel's work was displayed on an Asian sideboard. As Oskar Kaufmann had done, the designer of these two sideboards incorporated sculpture into the furniture. Here, however, the expressive movement is combined with Asian-inspired forms.

155   The Koch house, reception room with wax doll by Lotte Pritzel on top of the sideboard in a display case, Innendekoration, 1926

156 Lotte Pritzel at work, still from the movie
Die Pritzel Puppe, Deutsche Kunst und Dekoration, 1923

157 Lotte Pritzel, wax dolls,
Deutsche Kunst und Dekoration, 1911

158 Lotte Pritzel, wax doll,
Deutsche Kunst und Dekoration, 1920

159 Detail of the
two-door sideboard fig. 154

160 Lotte Pritzel, wax doll,
Deutsche Kunst und Dekoration, 1920

161 | 162   Unknown, salon table, carved and lacquered
wood, Berlin, circa 1913, private collection

163   Paul Ludwig Troost (August 17, 1878–January 21, 1934),
buffet in a dining room, Deutsche Kunst und Dekoration, 1911

The cantilevered table top rests on a square display case with Chinese latticework and large rounded corners in the Roman style.[8] Troost also used this corner solution and combined it with sculptural neoclassical carvings as can be seen on furniture by Johann Conrad Bromeis (1788–1855) at Museum Fasanerie in Fulda. It is this very table, by an as of yet unidentified creator, that shows what the impact of Berlin Deko on the shard of time under discussion reads like.

---

8   Lucien Zinutti, Il Linguaggio del Mobile Antico, Treviso, 2011, p. 340.

164   Max Wiederanders (September 16, 1890–November 28, 1976)
cabinet, lacquered wood, circa 1919, private collection

Unknown, vitrine, veneered birch, circa 1920, private collection

165   Fritz August Breuhaus (February 9, 1883–December 2, 1960),
bookcase, burled walnut veneer, manufactured by Hömig,
Hönnigen, 1924, private collection

166   Detail of fig. 165

167   Fritz August Breuhaus, library and living
room, Innendekoration, 1920

168   Paul Zucker, reception room,
Berlin, Moderne Bauformen, 1926

169 | 170   Fritz August Breuhaus
(February 9, 1883–December 2, 1960),
library table, burled walnut veneer, manufactured
by Hömig, Hönnigen, 1924, private collection

This model was originally displayed at the exhibition *Das Deutsche Buch* in 1919 and subsequently commissioned in 1924 for a private residence in Havixbeck, Westphalia. Breuhaus used modular repetition here in the horizontal direction, as did Paul Zucker (1891–1975) in his works, but also in the vertical direction, as did Matěj Blecha (1861–1919) in his lamp post of 1912[9] and Constantin Brâncuşi (1876–1957) in his Endless Column,[10] creating a tribute to infinity and the eternal.

9   Alexander Vegesack, Czech Cubism: Architecture, Furniture and Decorative Arts, New York, 1992, p. 114.

10   Radu Varia, Brancusi, New York, 2002, p. 237.

171 Unknown, cabinet, inlaid and stained flamed birch,
Berlin, circa 1925, private collection

172 Otto Firle
(14 October 1889–4 July
1966), cabinet, Berlin,
Innendekoration, 1924

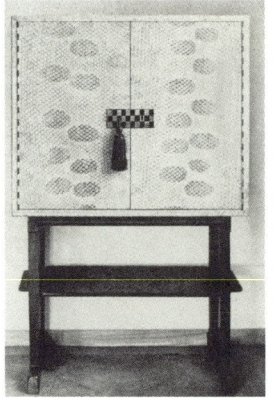

173 Haus & Garten
Vienna, cabinet,
snake skin,
Innendekoration, 1928

174   Unknown, commode, Macassar ebony,
carved and veneered, northern Germany, circa
1910, private collection

175   Bruno Paul (January 19, 1874–August 17, 1968),
Budapest armchair,, stained birch, manufactured by
Zoo-Werkstätten, Berlin, circa 1925, private collection

176　Jean Krämer (March 11, 1886–January 17, 1943), console table with desk unit, possibly for the reception room at the Otto Bing house, Berlin-Wannsee, walnut veneered, Berlin, 1921, private collection

177 | 178 Jean Krämer,
reception room for Otto Bing,
Berlin-Wannsee, Innendekoration, 1922

179   Oskar Kaufmann (February 2, 1873–September 8, 1956),
rendering for Café Schottenhaml, Berlin, 1926

THE REDISCOVERY OF GERMAN ART DECO

Decorative Arts during
the Weimar Republic (1918–1933)

Arne Sildatke

INTRODUCTION

At first, it may be hard to imagine that Art Deco and the Weimar Republic have anything in common. One is an art-historical label for the applied arts that originated in France and has had a lasting influence around the world, while the other is a short-lived period of Germany's troubled history in the twentieth century that conjures images of contemporary movements such as Bauhaus, tubular furniture, and the so-called Neue Sachlichkeit, or New Objectivity. Today, relatively few people are aware that in the 1920s, there was a German version of what is now called Art Deco, which shares specific roots with the French Art Déco and related to it in very inventive ways.[1] The phrase 'German Art Deco' must be regarded as an arbitrary construct, applied retroactively, as there was no contemporary unifying label connecting the various stylistic expressions of that period.

The term "Art Deco" was coined by art historians in reference to a style that flourished in France in the first third of the 20th century and developed a particularly decorative approach to the applied and fine arts. The term denotes a deliberate use of ornamentation that blends classical and exotic details.[2] Research in this narrow field, which began only recently, demonstrates that during this period a large number of German interiors were conceived in a spirit closely related to that of French Art Déco. This research finds that on both sides of the Rhine there was a shared wish to create a truly modern style with decorative aspects. The lack of research for so long on these stylistic developments may be due to the fact that the groundbreaking ideas of the Bauhaus and the movement's global triumph after World War II overshadowed all other expressions in the German applied arts that originated in the 1920s and earlier. As a result, it was long impossible to gain a comprehensive view of the Weimar Republic's artistic scene. Studies of the period had been deliberately over-simplified, especially in the field of design

---

[1] This article is based on my extensive research into Art Deco and German interior design during the Weimar Republic, see: Arne Sildatke, Dekorative Moderne. Das Art Déco in der Raumkunst der Weimarer Republik, Berlin/Münster 2013.

[2] For an overview of the different aspects of Art Deco see: Art Deco. 1910–1939 [exhibition cat. London 2003], edited by Charlotte Benton/Tim Benton/Ghislaine Wood, London, 2003. For a detailed discussion of the term "Art Deco" also see: Charlotte Benton/ Tim Benton, The Style and the Age, in ibid. pp. 13–27; Alastair Duncan, Art déco. Die Epoche, die Künstler, die Objekte, Munich, 2009; Pierre Kjellberg, Art Déco. Les maitres du mobilier, le décor des paquebots, Paris, 1986.

and the decorative arts. All artistic forms that did not fit into a simple paradigmatic scheme were regarded as minor digressions from what was presented as the more or less uniform unfolding path of modernism. The stylistic range of the Weimar Republic was in fact much more diverse than had been assumed earlier, with the radical avant-garde approach of the Bauhaus movement playing only a limited role in the everyday life and visual culture of that era. All along, until the very end of the decade, there was a confluence of contrasting artistic currents, fueled by newly gained liberties, the upbeat tempo of the metropolis, and both social and technological developments. There were open tensions among different positions, between the traditional and the revolutionary, and a coexistence of various styles and visual languages.

180   Cesar Pinnau (August 9, 1906–November 29, 1988), alcove with tea table, Moderne Bauformen, 1932

GERMAN ART DECO IN THE CONTEXT OF WEIMAR CULTURE AND THE DECORATIVE ARTS

Today, the period between 1918 and 1933 continues to attract extensive scholarly attention, perhaps in part because of the significant impact that the stereotypes with which it is associated have had on the collective cultural memory.[3] Until now art historical research into the decorative arts and interior design of this period in Germany has established a rigid model in which Expressionism and Neue Sachlichkeit function as the two main poles[4]: the evolution from early forms of Expressionism in home interior design towards avant-garde interiors influenced by Bauhaus and Neue Sachlichkeit has been described by some historians as a linear path that validates the paradigm of a functionalist modernism.

From this angle, Art Deco could be regarded as a kind of third option, situated somewhere between the two poles, and one that emerged from a reductive academic tradition. Art Deco is partly rooted in the cultural and stylistic tendencies of late Imperial Germany. The reform movement around 1900 was also an important milestone. In addition, the late 19th-century Kunstgewerbe movement, Jugendstil, and even "reform art" all tried to resolve the question of how the arts could remain relevant to the demands of a modern society. In Europe the debate was stoked by the emerging notion of an all-embracing unity of the arts—the *Gesamtkunstwerk*, or total work of art. This came to be seen as the highest ideal that would

---

[3]   One of the most recent international conferences dealing with the subject of the Weimar Republic, was programmatically named "Beyond Glitter and Doom. New Perspectives of the Weimar Republic", see: Jochen Hung, Beyond Glitter and Doom. New Perspectives of the Weimar Republic (H-Soz-u-Kult: Tagungsberichte), 2010, http://hsozkult.geschichte.hu-berlin.de/index.asp?pn=tagungsberichte&id=3387 (last accessed June 1, 2025).

[4]   See: Eberhard Kolb, Die Weimarer Republik, Munich, 2009, pp. 95–109.
This academic tradition is mainly influenced by Sigfried Giedion and his internationally esteemed book Space, Time and Architecture. The Growth of a New Tradition, Cambridge, MA 1941.

guarantee the unity of art and life, a goal so ardently desired as a remedy for the upheavals and shifts of the modern era that it was sought after well into the 1920s and beyond.

The visual culture of Weimar Germany (1918–1933) exhibited a rich array of exotic themes. Following the fashionable exoticism of the 19th century, the 1920s saw a resurgence of fascination with largely unknown cultures. This enthusiasm was particularly evident in interior design, where there was a widespread appetite for exotic motifs. Rather than striving for authentic reproductions of foreign lifestyles and their visual languages, these designs focused on the decorative adaptation of imaginative concepts. The goal was to blend exotic themes with elegant comfort and a certain refinement.

Whether applied in small-scale, private settings or in more grand, public situations, including cinemas and other entertainment venues, the depiction of the exotic was the subject of widely popular fascination. It was fueled by modern developments such as increasing tourism and faster transportation. Interest in the exotic comprises evolving concepts of cultural differences and a desire to affirm one's own culture. The use of special imagery also reflects shared Western ideas about the world, which were part of a longer tradition dating back to the 18th century.

When it came to private residences these fantastic exotic interiors took the form of luxurious architecture intended to evoke an exciting sense of the fashionable and the glamourous. The color schemes, furniture design, and material choices were steeped in the desire to create a synthesis of European traditions and the visual characteristics of more unfamiliar societies. Entertainment venues, including cinemas, theaters, cafés, and restaurants, were essential to the evolving mass culture in a highly urbanized context, incorporating specific adaptations of the exotic. These ephemeral spaces

served as refuges in an increasingly complex social environment. The "Cult of Distraction"[5] evolved into a pervasive element of the entertainment provided for a demanding mass audience.

The Art Deco movement in general, and especially its offshoots in Germany, was also under the influence of Viennese "reform art" from the beginning of the 20th century, namely the Wiener Werkstätte led by Josef Hoffmann and his colleagues. The success of the Wiener Werkstätte and its wide international appeal was a direct result of its 30-year commitment to a creative approach (1903–1932). These designers initiated innovative stylistic developments in the decorative arts that were enriched

181   Walter Sobotka (July 1, 1888–May 8, 1972), salon, Moderne Bauformen, 1926

by an intensive cross-cultural exchange between the two German-speaking capitals, Vienna and Berlin. This could be felt in the Austrian Pavilion

---

5   Siegfried Kracauer, Zerstreuung (1926), in: Das Ornament der Masse. Essays, Frankfurt am Main, 1977, p. 311.

at the Paris Exhibition in 1925, where the German architect Peter Behrens worked in coordination with Josef Hoffmann, who conceived the overall layout of the building.[6]

Beyond the definite influence of Wiener Werkstätte on German Art Deco, the origins of this style are actually quite complex and cannot be ascribed to a succession of epigones. One of its key formative moments was the German Werkbund Exhibition in Cologne,[7] which took place in 1914 as World War I was breaking out. It included work produced in Austria, some of which was from the Wiener Werkstätte. The exhibition was intended as an overview and summary presentation of the German Werkbund, founded in 1907 in the spirit of the aforementioned "reform movement." In addition to its modernist and functionalist heritage, this milestone exhibition already displayed what would become key features of a German Art Deco style that would blossom fully a decade later. The Werkbund Exhibition was devoted to searching for a contemporary, decorative style, which was seen as an agent of social bonding at a time when societal norms were becoming increasingly centered around the individual. From this perspective, a line can be drawn from this very early manifestation of German Art Deco to the 1925 Paris Exhibition (*Exposition des Arts Décoratifs et Industriels Modernes*), which later lent its name to the Art Deco style.[8]

KEY ASPECTS OF GERMAN ART DECO AND THE ARTISTS BEHIND IT

The pieces pictured in this publication represent the full range of the German Art Deco style and point to the trove of interior designs produced in Germany during the Weimar period and the years immediately preceding World War I. Many of these pieces share stylistic features with French Art Déco, yet they embody a distinctive style that underscores the complexity of Art Deco when viewed from a global perspective.[9]

German Art Deco interiors share several key aspects. Historians who have studied this period in depth have identified a number of distinct leitmotifs. One prominent motif is the reference to artistic tradition, with many interiors blending futuristic traits with traditional forms and ornamentation. Another recurring feature is the influence of German Expressionism, which was translated into decorative terms to function within the applied arts. This combination of factors contributed to the emergence of a new ornamental tradition, which was widely discussed among artists and designers of the time.[10] Behind their preoccupation with the question of ornamentation was a longing for an all-embracing contemporary style that would be widely appreciated and would revolve around a modern manifestation of ornamentation.

---

[6]   Besides Hoffmann and Behrens, there were works by nearly 300 artists in the exhibition. Behrens designed the pavilion's winter garden. He was selected to work on the Austrian Pavilion because of his position as a professor at the Viennese academy, where he succeeded Otto Wagner as the school dean. See: Hans-Joachim Kadatz, Peter Behrens Architekt, Maler, Grafiker und Formgestalter (1868–1940), Leipzig, 1977, pp. 49–50.

[7]   See: Die Deutsche Werkbund-Ausstellung Cöln 1914 [exhibition cat. Cologne 1984], edited by Wulf Herzogenrath, Cologne, 1984. Regarding the history of the German Werkbund see the catalog of the centennial exhibition in 2007: 100 Jahre Deutscher Werkbund. 1907–2007 [exhibition cat. Munich 2007], edited by Winfried Nerdinger, Munich, 2007. Joan Campbell, Der Deutsche Werkbund. 1907–1934, Stuttgart, 1981.

[8]   The name originated in the late 1960s and was coined by art historian Bevis Hiller in reference to the 1925 Paris exhibition: Bevis Hillier, Art Deco of the 20s and 30s, London, 1968, pp. 10-13.

[9]   For the international impact of Art Deco and its global manifestations see: Art Deco. 1910–1939 [see footnote 2], pp. 172-239, 325-343.

[10]   See: Wilhelm Michel, Stimmungswerte des expressionistischen Ornaments, in: Deutsche Kunst und Dekoration, issue 1, 1920, pp. 250-252. See also: María Ocón Fernández, Ornament und Moderne Theoriebildung und Ornamentdebatte im deutschen Architekturdiskurs (1850–1930), Berlin, 2003.

182   Hans Hartl (1899–1980), room for a lady, dated 1926,
Moderne Bauformen, 1927

and specific material qualities being emphasized to address both decorative and functionalist concerns.

Examples of French Art Déco are widely known through books and records of exhibitions. Over the years they have come to be seen as iconic, staking undisputed claim to the authorship of this style in academic publications and on the art market. It will take time before German objects and their designers achieve comparable recognition. This is likely to unfold as the result of a convergence of rigorous research and carefully planned exhibitions. We can start by shedding some light on the work of some of the most outstanding German Art Deco designers.

Perhaps pre-eminent among these designers is the architect Oskar Kaufmann (1873–1956). His Renaissance Theater in Berlin (built in 1926/27) is one of the very few extant masterworks of this kind of interior design.[11] By combining the jagged contours of Expressionism with Rococo-inspired forms, his work can be described as Expressionist Rococo, which has emerged as an essential facet of German Art Deco.[12] This symbiosis is further enhanced by exotic details that led Kaufmann to develop an extravagant—even exuberant—style in tune with contemporary tastes. He applied this style systematically to the design of fashionable entertainment venues, commercial interiors, and homes for the high bourgeoisie. Kaufmann cultivated a singular approach to decoration by combining stylized figurative elements with geometric forms. This blending of different visual languages was so prized by his wealthy patrons that Kaufmann became one of the most sought-after architects and interior designers of the 1920s.

In some cases, the use of softly flowing contours combined with shimmering fabrics evoked the Rococo boudoirs of the 18th century. Art Deco designers, like their predecessors, were captivated by distant cultures with an exotic allure. In the early 20th century, as global orientation and technological advances made access to distant cultures more feasible, designers eagerly infused interiors with these exotic influences. Additionally, some designs reflected echoes of Constructivism, Cubism, or De Stijl. Concepts of objectivity related to the Neue Sachlichkeit (New Objectivity) movement also found their way into interior design, with clear-cut shapes

[11]   For Kaufmann's work on the Renaissance Theater see: Antje Hansen: Oskar Kaufmann. Ein Theaterarchitekt zwischen Tradition und Moderne, Berlin, 2001, pp. 354–360. See also the contemporary article of the famous art critic Max Osborn about the brand-new theater: Max Osborn, Das "Renaissance-Theater" in Berlin. Eine Arbeit von Architekt Oskar Kaufmann – Berlin, in: Innendekoration, issue 8, 1927, pp. 298–310.

[12]   The expression was coined by the art historians and art critics Oscar Bie (1864–1938) and Max Osborn (1870–1946. See: Oscar Bie, Der Architekt Oskar Kaufmann, Berlin, 1928, pp. VIII, XI and Max Osborn, Oskar Kaufmann, Berlin, 1928.

183   Oskar Kaufmann (February 2, 1873–September 8, 1956)
and Eugen Stolzer (May 12, 1886–December 22, 1958),
foyer at the Renaissance Theater, Innendekoration, 1927

It may be useful to compare Kaufmann's career with that of his largely forgotten contemporary, Leo Nachtlicht (1872–1942), a very successful architect during the Weimar period who mostly built private homes. His luxurious interior designs from the first half of that era are closely related to Kaufmann's own.[13] Nachtlicht's attention to detail in his high-end furniture and objects has drawn praise from art critic Paul Westheim.[14] Nachtlicht's mixture of boldly articulated shapes with gently curved surfaces and soft fabrics is characteristic of the early phase of German Art Deco between 1920 and 1925. His interior designs from the early 1920s are exemplary of a billowing ornamental style that owes as much to Expressionist painting as to Rococo design. Our current ease with repurposing historic stylistic elements in new contexts makes it difficult to appreciate how novel it was at that time for

designers and architects to draw on the past in order to shape the future.[15] The evolution of traditional forms was seen as an opportunity to create a new style and to enable decoration to be understood in a new way. Thus, considerations of both past and future influenced the diverse approaches to interior design in the Weimar Republic.

In the latter half of the 1920s, Nachtlicht embraced a more cosmopolitan style, aligning more closely with the diverse international expressions of Art Deco. His later projects, such as the famous Haus Gourmenia (1929), a Berlin entertainment and restaurant venue, were designed for the pleasure of sophisticated urban patrons.[16] His designs began to place equal emphasis on geometric and figurative elements. They exemplified a distinctly elegant form of Neue Sachlichkeit and highlighted the decorative potential of materials with chrome-plated metal and glass. As can be seen in many venues devoted to leisure, such as theaters, cinemas and restaurants, Nachtlicht's projects during the late Weimar period reflect a more sensational and spectacular approach to Art Deco that embraces social desires and contradictions while expressing them in a decorative form.
The work of Emil Fahrenkamp (1885–1966) also typifies the German version of Art Deco. Fahrenkamp's furniture and interior designs were aligned with the overall concept of *Gesamtkunstwerk*, which focuses on the decorative staging of interior space. His early works included exotic details inspired by distant places or ancient cultures.[17] These designs could be described as Exotic Expression-

---

[13]   The same can be said about the architect Paul Zucker (1888–1971) and his work around 1920. See: Wolfgang Schäche/Norbert Szymanski, Paul Zucker. Der vergessene Architekt, Berlin, 2005.

[14]   See: Paul Westheim, Das Haus Dr. S. in Grunewald. Ein Umbau von Architekt Leo Nachtlicht, in: Innendekoration, issue 4, 1922, pp. 124–162.

[15]   See: Catharina Berents, Art Déco in Deutschland. Das moderne Ornament, Frankfurt am Main, 1997, pp. 17, 44–48.

[16]   For a further reading on this important project among Nachtlicht's works see the inaugural publication of Nachtlicht himself: Haus Gourmenia. Zur Eröffnung März 1929, edited by Leo Nachtlicht, Berlin, 1929. For a detailed research of the interior design see: Arne Sildatke [see footnote 1], pp. 358–362.

[17]   See e.g.: Heinrich Ritter, Form – Farbe – Lebensfreude. Zu den Arbeiten von Prof. Emil Fahrenkamp, in: Innendekoration, issue 12, 1921, pp. 360–368.

184   Leo Nachtlicht (August 12, 1872–September 22, 1942),
Weintraube restaurant, at Gourmenia-Haus, postcard, circa 1929

ism, which began to wane in the mid-1920s as he transitioned towards a more classical—and even rectilinear—elegance. Fahrenkamp intentionally employed modernist forms as embellishments and for ornamental interpretation. Contemporary observers criticized his drift away from functionalist modernism towards a fashionable decorative grammar as a surrender to the zeitgeist.[18] Although some critics may have had a point, we should not underestimate the integrative power of these designs. Their core strength lay in introducing a modern visual language to a broad audience. This not only captured interest but also, perhaps unintentionally, sparked discussions about the modern age among the newly urban masses. Unlike the leaders of other avant-garde movements, Art Deco designers did not set out to overturn tradition in a radical way. They developed an ability to communicate with discerning audiences, not in order to promote social reform or position themselves as moral authorities, but on a more subtle and playful level, which helped lay a foundation for future design trends. Designs of the period did exhibit a certain practicality and sobriety, but this was often a superficial formalism aimed at achieving visually pleasing and fashion-conscious results.

18   See: Laura Wilfinger, "My home is my castle" oder Brecht an Bord der Bauhaus?, in: An Bord der Bauhaus. Zur Heimatlosigkeit der Moderne, edited by Sonja Neef, Bielefeld, 2009, pp. 57–74. See also: Walter Dexel, Der Bauhausstil – ein Mythos (1964), in: Der Bauhausstil – ein Mythos: Texte 1921–1965, edited by Grete Dexel/Walter Vitt/Walter Dexel, Starnberg, 1976, pp. 17–20.76, pp. 17–20.

185   Emil Fahrenkamp (November 8, 1885–May 24, 1966),
bedroom for Schloß Walbeck,
Wasmuths Monatshefte für Baukunst, 1921

Whenever the budget permitted, German Art Deco featured a conspicuously excessive use of luxurious materials, decorative embellishments, and intricate layering. An example of this direction can be found in the projects of Fritz August Breuhaus de Groot (1883–1960) in the second half of the decade.[19] Academic research on Breuhaus's oeuvre produced the phrase "cultivated objectivity" (Kultivierte Sachlichkeit), which, in my mind, should be extended to "elegant objectivity" (Elegante Sachlichkeit) when referring to German Art Deco.

This brief overview of some of the most important practitioners of Art Deco in Germany barely scratches the surface of the whole subject. Many of the artists working in this particular style are long forgotten. Their alluring work remains to be discovered. Other architects such as Bruno Paul (1874–1968) or Paul László (1900–1993), while prominent, are seen as less committed to Art Deco in academic discourse. As a result, their important contributions to a decorative German style in the Weimar Republic are often forgotten or hardly noticed.[20]

[19]   See monograph on Breuhaus: Elisabeth Schmidle, Fritz August Breuhaus 1883–1960.
Kultivierte Sachlichkeit, Tübingen [et al.], 2006.

[20]   In the extensive literature on Bruno Paul you can find singular notions, connecting him with Art Deco. His interior design for the Weber apartment in Berlin (1914) has been mentioned in the past as the beginning of Art Deco in Germany. From the same perspective, Paul's Villa Bergmann in Dresden (around 1928) is regarded as the climax of his Art Deco period. See:
Alfred Ziffer (ed.), Bruno Paul. Deutsche Raumkunst und Architektur zwischen Jugendstil und Moderne, Munich, 1992, pp. 219–220, 252–253.

THE AFTERMATH AND LEGACY OF GERMAN ART DECO

There is no doubt that the Art Deco movement no longer had any effect on design in Germany after 1945. Already by the end of the Weimar Republic in 1933, when Hitler came to power, the fanciful and flamboyant Art Deco was relegated to a niche existence. Some of the artists, if they were Jewish or could be identified with any other group deemed unacceptable by the Nazis, were forced to leave Germany or were even murdered.[21] Others adapted to the new political order and chose to change their style. The official style of design in fashion after 1933 lacked any of the playful characteristics that were favored in the 1920s. The classical line in Art Deco had by then grown stiff and morphed into oppressive pathos. Even if some Art Deco designs continued to appear in the interiors of entertainment venues into the 1940s, the Allied bombings of Germany during the Second World War eradicated almost every trace of a style that was already vanishing. Globally, Art Deco features were increasingly integrated into modernism and the international style on account of their decorative qualities.

Art Deco was an important trend during the Weimar era and even for some time preceding it. Some of the work by artists such as Oskar Kaufmann and Emil Fahrenkamp demonstrate how quickly individual sensibilities can transform into collective ideas that trickle down into widely employed decorative patterns that incorporate stylized images of the exotic. German Art Deco shares many features with French Art Déco and should be seen in the context of an ongoing French-German intercultural exchange in the early twentieth century. Careful examination of the short-lived German Art Deco tradition reveals that some of its specific characteristics were already in evidence in the 1914 Werkbund exhibition in Cologne, which had a major impact on a very large audience as its essential features were disseminated through illustrated magazines, films and other media during the 1920s. In urban centers Art Deco gained momentum as it became part of a thriving visual culture that promoted indulgence in luxury, exoticism and elegance. Far from being an auxiliary cultural development in the early twentieth century, German Art Deco instead was a major phenomenon that peaked during the Weimar period but had already emerged in the preceding decade and continued to exert influence beyond 1933.

186   Fritz August Breuhaus
(February 9, 1883–December 2, 1960),
rendering, Moderne Bauformen, 1922

---

[21]   For more information about Jewish-German architects see the impressive dictionary by Myra Warhaftig: Deutsche jüdische Architekten vor und nach 1933. Das Lexikon. 500 Biographien, Berlin, 2005.

187　Oskar Kaufmann (February 2, 1873–September 8, 1956),
tier of the Renaissance Theater with intarsia by Cesar Klein,
Berlin, 1926

WHAT IS GERMAN ART DECO?

The Emergence of a New Period Style

Ulrich Leben

When looking at photographs of private interiors of the early 20th century, one is astonished to see how far our present-day idea of the period differs from the stylistic reality documented in these historic images. This observation may be confirmed by examining interiors in family albums, where the furniture and decorations once again diverge from those depicted in popular and avant-garde publications of the period itself, in which a nascent modernism seems to hold sway.[1]

Today, the image of interior and furniture design from the period between 1920 and 1933 is dominated by the second Bauhaus style, internationally known as modernism. In Germany, this style alone has been recognized and studied as the *sine qua non* of early 20th-century design. Only in recent years has a more complex stylistic view of the period emerged, revealing a moment when multiple tendencies coexisted. The dramatic, often explosive political and economic changes which occurred between 1910 and 1933 after a longer interlude of peace and economic growth, were most emphatically manifest in the creation of new residential areas in the industrial and administrative centers of German-speaking countries. In Germany, a young, optimistic, forward-looking, and bold generation was eager to display and explore its new social status, often with much more daring than in the established and more conservative societies of Austria, France, or England.

A surprising discovery in 21st-century hindsight is that interiors between 1910 and 1933 were markedly, even dominantly, inflected with historical styles. From what we see in period photographs, including those of family albums, the design of interiors and furniture was inspired by the reinvention and assimilation of historical styles, far more pervasively than by embracing—and inhabiting—the radical vision of what would be later known as modernism.[2]

This more moderate form of modernist design, still inscribed with the lineaments of historicism, has not yet been studied deeply enough in Germany; one is therefore tempted to name it "German Art Deco style."[3] This name is an adaptation of the designation for the Art Deco period in France, where the phenomenon has been recognized as a period style in its own right since the mid-20th century.

---

[1] Martha Huth, Berliner Lebenswelten der zwanziger Jahre. Bilder einer untergegangenen Kultur, Frankfurt am Main, 1996; Enno Kaufhold, Berliner Interieurs. Photographien von Waldemar Titzenthaler (1910–1930), Berlin, 1999.

[2] In Martha Huth's publication both visions co-exist, see footnote 1.

[3] Catharina Berents, Art Déco in Deutschland. Das moderne Ornament, Frankfurt, 1998.

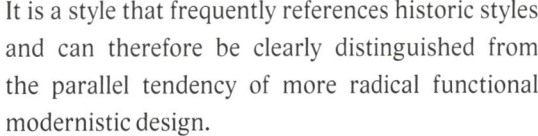

188   Friedrich Fehr (May 24, 1862–September 29, 1927), painting of the tea room at the Feinhals House, dated 1913, Moderne Bauformen, 1917

189   Bruno Paul (January 19, 1874–August 17, 1968), tea room for Josef Feinhals, 1911, Dekorative Kunst, 1912

It is a style that frequently references historic styles and can therefore be clearly distinguished from the parallel tendency of more radical functional modernistic design.

The French style was shaped by the 1925 Paris *Exposition Internationale des Arts Décoratifs et Industriels Modernes*, which showcased the antipodes of contemporary design. One was inspired by traditional style; the other by a more radical vision of modernity, which would culminate in Le Corbusier's modular apartments. The opposition of these two movements was recognized and commented on at the time.

In this context, the writings of the Berlin-based architect Paul Zucker, who later immigrated to New York, are relevant. As early as 1927, Zucker foresaw the limitations of the vision of Le Corbusier and his ilk, commenting, "He is going wrong when he thinks that the residential home can be a machine, as the airplane can be a transportation engine. The basic problem of architecture is to be defined at the

point where the purely engineered conception is part of a necessary whole, but this should not be the only directing force."

Zucker did not aim to create a "new style" to which every project must submit, but recommends that every project be treated as an individual case study, a unique response to its own design imperatives.[4] Since the mid-20th century, our view of the early modernist period has been a seamless narrative of lean lines and honest use of industrial materials—exhorted by the Bauhaus—a view successfully imposed by generations of art historians in the United States and Europe.

It also emerges clearly that the artistic movements of Symbolism, Expressionism, Cubism, Surrealism and even the spiritualism espoused by Kandinsky, for example, influenced architecture and the applied arts as vehemently as the much more conservative aesthetic, characterized by the use of traditional crafts, folk arts, and references to historic style. All these often oppositional manifestations of a

---

4   Wolfgang Schäche/Norbert Szymanski, Paul Zucker – Der vergessene Architekt, Berlin, 2005, pp. 77.

190   Edmund Körner (December 2, 1874–February 14, 1940),
armchair for Carl Herzberg, Macassar ebony,
Essen, 1911, Espace Emmanuel Eyraud, Paris

191   Edmund Körner, music room for Carl Herzberg,
Essen, 1911, Moderne Bauformen 1914

design ethos coexisted, even if the more conservative strains did not receive the same publicity as the nascent International Style.

For some years after World War I, Germany did not participate in international exhibitions. In fact, Germany was invited very late to the 1925 *Exposition Internationale des Arts Décoratifs et Industriels Modernes* in Paris, and decided not to participate. However, there were national exhibitions in German-speaking countries that addressed the decorative arts within the geographic space of what had been the German and Austrian Empires.[5]

In 1914, the Werkbund Exhibition in Cologne was the last exhibition of international significance to attract international attention to German design. After the advent of World War I such events were replaced by periodicals and publications on con-

temporary interior and furniture design, aesthetic ideas largely distributed and communicated by German architects, designers, and stage designers. They were aimed at both a national and international audience, as can be assumed from a number of editions containing texts in English, French, or Italian. In this context, the publication houses of Julius Hoffmann in Stuttgart and Alexander Koch in Darmstadt are particularly valuable. Their books are the only trace of many interiors and furnishings which no longer exist.[6]

Starting in the early 2000s, new research by a young generation of art historians begun radically to revise the perspective on the period. Today, research is facilitated by electronic media and digitized reproductions of publications and periodicals. The period from 1915 to 1933 leaves many questions open, but the published material attests to the existence

5   Alexander Koch, Das neue Kunsthandwerk in Deutschland und Oesterreich unter Berücksichtigung der Deutschen Gewerbeschau München, Darmstadt, 1923.

6   A good number of lavishly illustrated periodicals and books were presented by the publication houses of Julius Hoffmann in Stuttgart and Alexander Koch in Darmstadt. Today these are the most important resources for research on the subject.

192   Vereinigte Werkstätten, sideboard, lacquered wood and granite top, circa 1920, private collection

of all the variegated tendencies one observes in Germany's European neighboring countries.[7]

With the beginning of the century and in their conception of the *Gesamtkunstwerk*, artists such as Peter Behrens, Henry van de Velde, and Richard Riemerschmid began creating furniture and decorations for unique, specific sites. Today, identifying surviving fragments of these interiors is possible only through comparison with photographs. Because of this deracination, appreciating individual surviving elements of these works has become a complex matter. German design from before 1933 presents a fractured vision, given the successful annihilation of artistic innovation by Nazi persecution, followed by the physical destruction of war and the deliberate academic eradication by subsequent generations. We are left, like archaeologists, to reassemble the fragments of this incalculably rich cultural period in Germany.[8]

Which types of design were most appreciated by contemporaries, and how widely were they distributed, in elite commissions as well as in mass-produced consumer goods of a more ephemeral character? How did these types manifest in the designs of a generation of designers, who were highly educated and acutely aware of the chronology of historic styles, which they assimilated in a sophisticated way into interiors in Berlin, Breslau, Cologne, Düsseldorf, Frankfurt, and Munich?

To discern which particular historic styles influenced the period, one needs to be able decipher the formal language employed for each of them. Only in recent years has this process of identification taken shape, allowing for the rediscovery of many items that had fallen into near oblivion for at least two generations. The reunification of Germany has made numerous surviving artifacts available, enhancing and broadening our appreciation of the period.

---

[7]   A very good example is the publication on the imaginary Landhaus Sankt Antonius, published by Alexander Koch in 1918: Fritz Ostini, Das Landhaus "Sankt Antonius." Ein Künstlertraum, Darmstadt, 1918.

[8]   Many surviving buildings and interiors were taken down or destroyed in the rage of rebuilding a new Germany, which deliberately wanted to cut all links with its past. One of the first publications dedicated to one architect is the research done by Alfred Ziffer (ed.), Bruno Paul. Deutsche Raumkunst und Architektur zwischen Jugendstil und Moderne, Munich, 1992.

193　Else Wenz-Viëtor (April 30, 1882–May 29, 1973),
tea room for the Werkbund Exhibition, Cologne, 1914,
Moderne Bauformen, 1914

A high level of interest in design and the rigorous education of architects and designers ensured familiarity with the chronological organization of European historic styles, meticulously developed by art historians in the latter part of the 19th century. This allowed designers to understand "style" systematically, as a logical historic succession from Classicism—Biedermeier in Germany—to the Eclecticism of the late 19th century. The dissemination of this knowledge was supported by the proliferation of decorative arts museums and craft and design schools, and was documented in numerous publications. Luxurious editions targeted the upper-class market, while affordable versions also reached industrial workers and art students. Powerful political interest in design education for the lower and working classes had actually proven to be a success. It is therefore not surprising to find architects such as Emil Fahrenkamp in Düsseldorf or Bruno Paul in Munich, adroitly referencing French Louis XVI, German Biedermeier, or earlier historic styles in their furniture design.

Between 1910 and 1915, one discovers German projects that are cognate to the works of Paris-based decorator and designer Georges Hoentschel and his follower Armand Rateau. Both aimed to regenerate contemporary design by drawing inspiration from historic French styles, particularly from the very fashionable later 18th century. By twisting historic inspiration into something new, the aim of their sophisticated designs was to ensure contemporary design that possessed the material excellence of craftsmanship, an enduring hallmark of fine French furniture and objects.[9]

The honest use of simple or even man-made materials, such as plywood for furniture or stamped metals for hardware (fig. 174), characterizes German design of the period. In contrast to the luxurious productions of Parisian designers and workshops, even pieces aimed at an elite German clientele employed industrial materials. Chosen primarily for their low cost, these materials give German design a distinctive character—often perceived as "German" due to their humble materiality, which can hinder their appreciation today.

194　Ottomar Starke (June 21, 1886–August 8, 1962),
set design for Shakespeare's *Julius Caesar* in the tent
of Brutus, Dekorative Kunst, 1913

In Germany, as in France and England, historic trends such as Chinoiserie, Orientalism, and other Exoticisms were known and adapted. Frequently it was in national prototypes such as historic residences that such exotic conceits were used; they would have been recognized easily by everybody. Architects consciously drew from these examples,

9　Danielle Kisluk-Grosheide/Deborah L. Krohn/Ulrich Leben, Salvaging the Past. Georges Hoentschel and French Decorative Arts from The Metropolitan Museum, The Bard Graduate Center, The Metropolitan Museum, New York/New Haven/London, 2013 Franck Olivier/François Rateau, Armand Albert Rateau, Paris, 1992.

195 Peter Behrens (April 14, 1868–February 27, 1940),
Meirowsky house, Cologne, Innendekoration, 1911

1920 and 1926, for the Berlin-based industrialist Herbert Max Gutmann. The space featured a fresco by Rudolf Hengstenberg depicting the Gutmann children engaged in sports. The gymnasium could, on occasion, be transformed into a movie theater. The ogival ceiling arches may have been influenced by the Great Halls on the top floors of English country houses from the Tudor period.[10]

One of the early examples of Gothic revival of the period was the renovation, again by Hans Poelzig, of the former winter home of Circus Schumann in Berlin, for use as a theater. In transforming the building, Poelzig clearly referred to ecclesiastical buildings from the Gothic age in order to create a building that would attract huge crowds of people to theatrical or cinema presentations. The latter were envisaged as popular attractions serving a new age, just as the religious monoliths of Gothic cathedrals had magnetized the devout masses.[11]

The artificial silk girl, the main character in Irmgard Keun's book of the same title, visits one of her courtiers, who is dressed in a Kimono and has his flat furnished with authentic low-standing Japanese furniture, with mattresses as seating.[12] Photographs, which Waldemar Titzenthaler took in the Berlin apartment of Fritz Lang and his wife for the magazine *Die Dame*, reveal authentic Asian furniture and artworks, evidence of the embrace of alternative forms of habitation in the 1920s in Berlin, just as in Paris or London.[13]

Exposure to authentic ethnologic artifacts and motifs often influenced European artists, who introduced them into their own works. The painter Ernst Ludwig Kirchner, who split from the Expressionist artist group Die Brücke in 1912 and moved to Berlin, decorated his atelier there with paintings inspired by Oceanic or African art.

creating contemporary interpretations of ancient motifs by translating them into a modern idiom. One heavily referenced style was Gothic, which Hans Poelzig successfully reinvented for the stage set of the 1920 film *The Golem*. Poelzig reconstructed the former ghetto of Prague with medieval architectural references and expressionistic broken lines. Gothic elements were also favored by set designers for early movies, where the scenery of old German towns alluded both to the broken lines of Expressionist painters and to medieval Gothic features. The effect was striking rather than "traditional."

A significant surviving example of early 20th-century German historicism is the gymnasium designed by Reinhold Mohr for the Villa Gutmann, also known as Herbertshof, in Potsdam, between

10   Vivian J. Rheinheimer, Herbert M. Gutmann. Bankier in Berlin, Bauherr in Potsdam, Kunstsammler. Leipzig, 2007.

11   Heike Hambrock, Bauen im Geist des Barock. Hans und Marlene Poelzig, Berlin/Delmenhorst, 2005, pp. 31–41.

12   Irmgard Keun, Das kunstseidene Mädchen, Berlin, 1932.

13   Enno Kaufhold [see footnote 1], p. 9 fig. 2; p. 22 fig. 12.

Expressionism had its impact upon interior design through the use of vibrant color schemes, with painters drawing inspiration from German folk art, which had already been applied to commercial design in the annual publications of the Werkbund. In the compositions by artists of Die Brücke these colors were often inspired by experiences of outdoor life, or, in contrast, of the frenetic rhythm of the metropolis with its social diversity and cityscape rapidly changing through motorization and industrialization. The artist Wassily Kandinsky, who had been a member of the artist group Der Blaue Reiter, used inspiration from the folk art of Russia, his country of origin. While living in Munich, he painted the paneling and furniture of the Murnau cottage of his friend, the painter Gabriele Münter, with Russian folk motifs in vibrant colors. Kandinsky would persevere in his analysis of colors based on the *Farbenlehre* of Johann Wolfgang von Goethe. Goethe's theories resonated in the early 20th century, influencing compositions of contrasting colors, which Kandinsky later transmuted into wallpaper designs when he taught at the Bauhaus.[14]

Another artist's work is a colorfully visionary group of wall paintings by Wenzel Hablik, only recently rediscovered in his private house in Itzehoe, worth mentioning for its uniquely decorative scheme.

Built Expressionism can be found in the broken lines of the angular front of Fritz Höger's Chilehaus in Hamburg from 1924, as well as in the hall of the Grassi Museum in Leipzig, built by Zweck and Voigt in 1925–1928. Tendencies towards a cosmic vision and new spirituality were instigated by writer-mystics such as Rudolf Steiner, the founder of anthroposophy. Steiner, himself, was very interested in the study of Goethe's *Farbenlehre*. Since the turn of the century these studies and preoccupations opened the way to new artistic visions that would permeate architecture and interiors.

196   Hans Poelzig (April 30, 1869–June 14, 1936), sketch for *The Golem*, 1920, Wasmuths Monatshefte für Baukunst, 1925

Bruno Taut's shimmering, faceted Glass Pavilion, shown at the 1914 Werkbund Exhibition in Cologne, was perhaps the apotheosis of Expressionism in architecture, a temporary structure which would nevertheless exert a seminal influence upon architecture and interior design after World War I. While the building was a prototype for new ways of using glass in architecture, Taut saw glass as a material analogue to human emotion and spirituality. He was inspired by the writer Paul Scheerbart, whose aphorisms about glass and color—such as "Colored glass destroys hatred"—Taut had inscribed on the lintels of the Glass Pavilion's walls. The many-faceted glass dome, lit from the inside, would be compared to the internal glow of an ardent crystal.

Examples of the subtle use of indirect light sources in an interior include the counter hall of the publishing house Hannoverscher Anzeiger by Fritz Höger from 1927/28 and the staircase of the Pressa building designed by Erich Mendelsohn for the publishing house of Rudolf Mosse in 1928 in Cologne.

14   Renate Scheper, Farbenfroh! Colourful!, Berlin, 2005.

197　Cesar Klein (September 14, 1876–March 13, 1954),
intarsia at the Renaissance Theater, Berlin, 1926

When the filmmaker Fritz Lang visited New York in 1924 he had his first encounter with skyscrapers, which impelled his soaring stage sets, notably in the movie Metropolis, produced between 1925–27. Eugen Schüftlan created the decorations, which are synonymous with a futuristic or visionary mode of the Art Deco style of the period. Echoes of Metropolis still reverberate in the later twentieth century post-modern works of the Italian designer Ettore Sottsass, founder of the Memphis group.

It is only very slowly that artists' names re-emerge. Many practitioners were forced to leave the country mid-career due to the persecution of the National Socialist regime, and then forgotten, their works frequently disfigured or destroyed in the course of World War II. By chance, the very forward-looking interiors of Villa Sommerfeld, built by Walter Gropius and Adolf Meyer in 1921, today destroyed, are well documented through photographs. They

show a new use of structural and decorative wooden elements, with an expressionistic carved staircase rail by Joost Schmidt and stained glass windows by Josef Albers. Such intact documentation is a rare case, for most of the designers and craftsmen have been forgotten.

One significant rediscovery is the intarsia design by artist Cesar Klein for the Renaissance Theater in Berlin Charlottenburg, built in 1926 by Oskar Kaufmann.[15] The works are influenced by Expressionist as well as Neo-Rococo elements, and constitute today one of the best-preserved and iconic examples surviving from the period. The recently restored color schemes of the theater's bar and lounge convey a vivid impression of one of the most influential designers of his time. The paneling was done in marquetry by the Berlin-based enterprise of Ernst Nast.

In a recent sale, there appeared a chest of drawers after a design by Cesar Klein and Michael Rachlis, originally commissioned for the villa of the industrialist Avram Zissu. This piece of furniture exemplifies perfectly the integration of new design ideas applied to marquetry.[16]

During the initial period of the Bauhaus, founded in Weimar in 1919 under the direction of Walter Gropius, the "Vorkurs"[17] taught by Johannes Itten was an influential introductory course designed to prepare students for the diverse and experimental curriculum. It was at this time that experiments with developing a line of furniture production began. The early pieces show the influence of folk and ethnic cultures, of which some examples may be seen in the Bauhaus Archiv in Berlin.[18] For example, the first piece of furniture ever designed by Marcel Breuer,

---

[15]　Antje Hansen, Oskar Kaufmann: Ein Theaterarchitekt zwischen Tradition und Moderne (Die Bauwerke und Kunstdenkmäler von Berlin), Berlin, 2001, p. 108.

[16]　Auction No. 217, Galerie Pels Leusden, Villa Grisebach, Berlin, 28 November 2013, lot 340.

[17]　Itten's "Vorkurs" emphasized fundamental principles of design, color theory, and material studies, encouraging students to explore their creativity and develop a solid understanding of basic artistic and architectural concepts. This course laid the groundwork for the Bauhaus's innovative approach to art and design education, blending theory with hands-on practice.

[18]　Bauhaus-Möbel, A Legend Reviewed, Bauhaus Archiv, Berlin, 2002.

in 1919, was the African chair, along with some pine cabinets painted with expressionistic motifs in vibrant colors.

The decisive shift to a commercially sustainable line of furniture production was only realized after 1923, following Walter Gropius's falling out with Johannes Itten, which ultimately led to Itten's resignation. Driven by the idea of launching a line of production that could be industrially produced and targeted at larger groups of consumers, Gropius abolished traditional workshop-oriented production in favor

198   Michael Rachlis (July 29, 1884–1953), commode for Abraham Leib Zissu, intarsia by Cesar Klein, 1929, private collection

of industrial fabrication based on standardized elements. Although this mode of production did not prove very successful for Gropius by the time he left the Bauhaus in 1928, the 1930 Werkbund Exhibition in Paris provided an opportunity for him and some of his former colleagues to present their modern view of Germany to an international audience. It later led to the development of the readymade "flat-pack" furniture of the present day.

Embracing industrial production paved the way for modernism, which continues to dominate our image of the period. Fresh research projects and evolving perspectives promise to reveal a far more diverse and complex history of design aesthetics and practice from the first third of the 20th century.

199   Walter Gropius (May 18, 1883–July 5, 1969), staircase for Adolf Sommerfeld, 1920, Wasmuths Monatshefte für Baukunst, 1922/23

200 | 201 | 202   Oskar Kaufmann (February 2, 1873–September 8, 1956),
bathroom for Leo Lewin, Giallo di Siena marble, sculptural works by Franz Metzner (1870–1919),
mosaics by Cesar Klein (1876–1954), manufactured by Puhl & Wagner Gottfried Heinersdorf

A MODERN TEMPLE OF ART

Leo Lewin's Villa in Breslau[1]

Magdalena Palica

"The house I would like to return to"
Georg Kolbe, 16.03.1921[2]

The years of the Great War (1914–1918) took an enormous toll on European culture. Its all-encompassing nature even consumed philosophers, who were recruited to lend their talents to national propaganda programs—an effort dubbed "The War of Philosophers" by Peter Hoeres[3]—which painters were then expected to translate into political posters and writers into leaflets. Most of the artists who did not want to support such nationalist endeavors ended up serving in the trenches. By 1917, the war had already destroyed many talented people and more would die within the following year. Even in the midst of such loss to the artistic community, the war at times offered an opportunity for a spectacular *Gesamtkunstwerk* to emerge. One shining example is the villa that a 36-year-old Jewish entrepreneur named Leo Lewin decided to purchase in Breslau in 1917 and redecorate with the ambitious goal of turning it into a modern temple of art.

A year earlier, the artistic milieu of Breslau had been nearly wiped out with the loss of two personalities vital to its cultural identity: the death of renowned physician Albert Neisser, whose villa housed a delightful collection of art, and the relocation to Dresden of local architect Hans Poelzig, director of Breslau's Academy of Art and Design. After Neisser's death, his villa was converted into a museum and the city lost one of its most important meeting places for artists and their admirers. Poelzig's predilection for modern artistic movements had exerted significant influence on the rather conservative tastes of the local society, and with his move to Dresden avant-garde art lost an essential supporter in the capital of Lower Silesia.

The income that allowed Leo Lewin to even imagine his project came from the textile company, C. Lewin, which had been founded by his father, Carl Lewin, and was one of a handful of army contractors to benefit from mass orders for military uniforms thanks to the war. By 1916, Leo was co-managing the business, together with his father and two brothers, Salo and Max. The prosperity of such contractors stood in sharp contrast to the vast majority of businesses in Breslau that had been forced to cut

---

[1] The article is based on my research about Jewish art collectors in Breslau, see: Magdalena Palica, Od Delacroix do van Gogha. Żydowskie kolekcje sztuki w dawnym Wrocławiu (From Delacroix to van Gogh. Jewish Collections of Art in Breslau), Wrocław, 2010, and Magdalena Palica, Von Delacroix bis van Gogh. Jüdische Kunstsammlungen in Breslau, in: Jüdische Leben in Schlesien zwischen Ost und West, edited by Anno Herzig, Göttingen, 2014, pp. 390–406.

[2] Note on the page from Leo Lewin guest book. Georg-Kolbe-Museum, Berlin Nachlass Georg Kolbe, Signatur GK.608; 21; 1; 1.

[3] P. Hoeres, Der Krieg der Philosophen. Die deutsche und britische Philosophie im Ersten Weltkrieg, Paderborn, 2004.

their production to conserve fuel in the midst of coal shortages during an unusually harsh winter. These shortages had forced Germany to become the first country in the world to implement daylight-saving time. Also contributing to Breslau's economic hardship were poor autumn harvests and the British naval blockade, the combination of which had led to drastic food shortages for the entire country. The Lewin family's growing affluence during World War I enabled its members to spend significant sums of money on art.

It was probably around 1916 that Leo Lewin's passion for art blossomed, undoubtedly inspired in part by Neisser's collection and villa, which served as a common meeting place for local artists, collectors, and critics. Lewin was hardly the only wealthy Jewish art collector from Breslau to become one of the leading promoters of new trends in art around that time.[4] Among others were Carl Sachs, the owner of the one of the biggest collections of modern art in Breslau (including paintings by Monet, Courbet, Delacroix and Pissarro);[5] Hugo Kolker, a great admirer of Edvard Munch and Henri Matisse; and Hugo Naphtali, whose daughter Annie was one of the first women in the city to study the history of art. Neisser's house, often at the center of this community, had been built by Hans Griesbach, whose exquisite interiors were designed by Fritz Erler. Decorated with masterpieces of art, it was a model for what Leo Lewin hoped to achieve in the following years.

In 1917 Carl Lewin decided to commission a series of portraits by the renowned German painter Max Liebermann. Those paintings, along with bust sculptures by Georg Kolbe, were gifts for Carl's children. One of the first paintings in Leo Lewin's collection was a large canvas by Liebermann that depicted his father. Liebermann became one of Leo Lewin's favorite artists, and Lewin came to own

at least 16 of his paintings and more than 40 of his drawings. Among these were portraits of Lewin's wife, Helen, whose delicate face can also be found in the works of painter Max Slevogt, who portrayed her multiple times.

203   Oskar Kaufmann (February 2, 1873–September 8, 1956), Max Slevogt, table for Leo Lewin, carved rosewood and mosaic top, private collection, Berlin

In 1917 Max Slevogt was at the pinnacle of his career. After the outbreak of World War I, he had been sent to the western front as an official portraitist of the war, but three years later he was recalled to Berlin to become the director of a master studio in the Royal Academy of the Arts. Two decades younger than Liebermann and more inclined towards modern tastes, Slevogt became a friend and advisor to Lewin. Aware of the collector's passion for horse breeding, he designed Lewin's ex libris with an equestrian motif. He also sketched portraits of Lewin and the two men even spent a summer vacation together.

Lewin's villa at Akazienallee 12, bought with the intention of displaying his growing collection of art, was in the fashionable neighborhood of Kleinburg, which had been absorbed into Breslau's city limits by the end of the 19th century. The most prestigious part of this district was the estate of villas adjacent

4   Małgorzata Stolarska-Fronia, Jewish Art Collectors from Breslau and Their Impact on the City's Cultural Life at the End of the 19th and the Beginning of the 20th Century, in: Jüdische Sammler und ihr Beitrag zur Kultur der Moderne, edited by Annette Weber, Heidelberg, 2011, pp. 237–253.

5   The admiration must have been mutual since Carl Sachs also owned a print portrait of Leo Lewin by Max Slevogt.

204   Max Slevogt
(October 8, 1868–September 20, 1932),
mosaic table top, manufactured by
Puhl & Wagner Gottfried Heinersdorf

to the Southern Park in Wrocław. Only two blocks separated Lewin's new home from the house of Carl Sachs, perhaps the city's most important art collector. The home of Lewin's father was also nearby at Akazienallee 17–19.[6] Leo Lewin's villa had been built a decade earlier by Breslau architect Richard Ehrlich (1866–1931) in a simple architectural style for Consul Fritz Ehrlich, whose taste leaned towards the classical. Believing the villa's interiors to be ill–suited to the modern temple of art he envisaged, Lewin secured the services of renowned architect Oskar Kaufmann to redecorate them. That in itself was a stroke of luck: Kaufmann had previously designed important public buildings in Germany, mostly theaters, but the dearth of big commissions during the war compelled him to gladly accept requests to redecorate private houses.

It is very likely that the main theme of the villa's interior makeover came from Max Slevogt. A round mosaic table top that he designed in 1917 for the villa[7]—the mosaic technique was typical of Roman art—depicts a bacchanalian procession of characters from different times and places. The dancing figures included putti and a harlequin, musicians, naked women, and wild animals. Depictions of music and dance were to become a leitmotif in the design of Lewin's house.

---

[6]   After Carl Lewin died the building was modernized by Richard Ehrlich for Leo's brother Max.

[7]   The large drawing in tempera technique (101 cm in diameter) was a part of Lewin's collection and was auctioned at Cassirer & Helbing in Berlin in 1927. Sammlung Leo Lewin Breslau. Deutsche und Französische Meister des XIX. Jahrhunderts. Gemälde, Plastik, Zeichnungen, Paul Cassirer und Hugo Helbing, Berlin, 1927, lot 145.

205   Detail of mantelpiece and library frame in the study

The stunning table top attracted attention during the manufacturing process at Puhl & Wagner, the largest German producer of glass mosaics and stained glass. In early February 1919 Gottfried Heinersdorff, director of Puhl & Wagner, wrote to Oskar Kaufmann that the piece should be ready by the end of that month, adding that many of the manufacturer's other customers were very interested in seeing the final product. Heinersdorff suggested an ideal opportunity to unveil the mosaic to the public—an exhibition of Roman mosaics scheduled to open shortly thereafter at the Gurlitt gallery in Berlin. It is not certain whether the table was ultimately exhibited at Gurlitt's as there was a dispute over its price, which had increased from an estimated 19,500 mark to the huge amount of 34,500 mark, likely because of unforeseen problems in executing the design. Heinersdorff wrote that "in our 25 years of practice we never had a piece nearly as complicated as this one," which clearly did not make Lewin happy.

Kaufmann and his collaborator, Expressionist painter Cesar Klein, must have welcomed the musical theme as the dominant motif of Lewin's redecorated villa; prior to then, the work of both men had mainly focused on theatrical interiors and scenic design. It is worth mentioning that Kaufmann had designed houses before 1917 for luminaries of the German musical world such as composer Victor Holländer and musicologist Werner Wolffheim, none of which featured interiors as heavily laden with musical references as those in Lewin's villa in Breslau. This suggests that the dominance of the musical iconography was per Lewin's request. Slevogt was a gifted singer and pianist, and an admirer of Wagner and Mozart. Kaufmann was a skillful pianist himself and is on record as having stated that he had once wanted to become a musician, which could explain why Lewin's request for a dominant musical theme was greeted so enthusiastically.[8] The artists used motifs from various cultures, from Japan and China to Africa and Germany, but the small figures present on the furniture, mosaics, and lamps had one thing in common: they were all dancing. The musical theme extended to numerous art pieces that Lewin commissioned once the interiors had been completed. One of them, known as *The Lute Player* and designed around 1920 by sculptor Ernst Barlach, had been intended for the villa's main hall.[9] For that same space Lewin commissioned the sculptures *Reading Monks*, *Rest on the Flight into Egypt* and *Prodigal Son*.

206   Oskar Kaufmann (February 2, 1873–September 8, 1956), light fixture for an entrance

The round vestibule where the Barlach sculptures were to be displayed was decorated with ceramic depictions of riders and running animals, as well as a huge lamp adorned with figurines of dancing women. For the game room, Kaufmann designed a table whose top surface depicted a theatrical

---

8   Many photographs of the interiors were published by Oscar Bie in: Oscar Bie, Der Architekt Oskar Kaufmann, Berlin, 1928.

9   Ernst Barlach. Werke und Werkentwürfe aus fünf Jahrzehnten, edited by Maria Rüger, Berlin, 1981, pp. 121–122.

207   Oskar Kaufmann, study for Leo Lewin, on the wall a portrait of Konrad Fiedler by Hans von Marées

scene sketched by Cesar Klein.[10] That room also featured tall stained glass windows (fig. 14) that displayed colorful scenes of people from various cultures, including Chinese and Turks, playing such games as chess, dominoes, and cards. Lewin's choice of decoration for the study reflected his passion for horse breeding; just a couple of years later he would buy Gestüt Römerhof, the top stud farm in the Weimar Republic. The equestrian motifs were everywhere: a big relief plate over the marble fireplace depicted a rider; small figures of hunters and horses ornamented desk-sets and lamps; and a huge semicircular desk was covered with intarsia of Chinese motifs designed by Cesar Klein. Elaborate decoration was sometimes to be found in rather unexpected places such as the backs of cabinet doors, which in one case featured a fine composition in intarsia depicting a faun as a personification of singing, a naked man holding grapes signifying wine, and a dancing woman, all of which were clearly inspired by paintings by Max

Slevogt. The house's signature art piece, however, was a big Steinway piano decorated by Kaufmann himself. It was a splendid instrument. The case was ebonized while its barrel-shaped legs were carved with silhouettes of small figures playing accordions and bagpipes among blooming plants, exhibiting a combination of figurative elements and geometric forms perfected by Kaufmann. Even the nursery and the bathroom were decorated. In 1928 Oscar Bie, Kaufmann biographer, reported, "Not a doorknob, curtain, or a lamp was left unattended."[11]

For all the opulence of its interior design, the villa's central purpose was to serve as a showcase for Leo Lewin's fast-growing art collection. Kaufmann took great care to ensure that not only the paintings but also small sculptures and works on paper such as drawings and pastels were exhibited properly. He designed tiny cabinets and niches suitable for presenting various works of art.

Kaufmann realized that the decoration could be overwhelming and that only perfect alignment of all the elements would create an impression of harmony. The redecorated interiors were admired by many visitors, including Max Slevogt himself. Critics who wrote about the interiors after 1945, having seen the designs only in photographs (after the house had been stripped of its decoration) sometimes found them excessively sumptuous and even artistically questionable.[12] Such unfavorable judgments probably reflected the inability of photographs to capture either the beauty of the elaborate details or the perfect harmony achieved among all of the design elements. In recent years, pieces of furniture from Lewin's villa have started to appear on the art and antiques markets. All of them, from the majestic Steinway piano to a small lamp, exhibit intricate details that complement one another perfectly.

10   Die Weltkunst, issue 59, 1989, p. 402.

11   Oscar Bie, [see footnote 8], p. XI.

12   Antje Hansen, Oskar Kaufmann. Ein Theaterarchitekt zwischen Tradition und Moderne (Die Bauwerke und Kunstdenkmäler von Berlin), Berlin, 2001, pp. 37, 300.

208   Oskar Kaufmann (February 2, 1873–September 8, 1956), cabinet in the games room

By 1921, the house was ready to be presented to the public. Among its illustrious guests were sculptor Georg Kolbe and philosopher Ernst Cassirer, as well as the art critic Karl Scheffler, who described his visit enthusiastically in the widely read art magazine *Kunst und Künstler*: "The walls are covered with the most beautiful works of German and French artists. The most valuable prints, both old and modern, are abundant. One is shown rarities not often found in even the biggest print cabinets, which includes two drawings by Rembrandt. [...] Vitality reigns everywhere. And this vitality pours out of the collection to spread among the art-loving circles of the city."[13]

Financial problems prevented Lewin from completing his ambitious project. He decided not to buy the sculptures of Barlach for the main hall (Barlach sold them as independent pieces). The swan fountain by famed sculptor August Gaul was installed in the villa's garden, but the infrastructure to connect it to a water source was never built.[14] Other works of art commissioned by Lewin, including the big orangutan sculpture by Gaul (bought in 1925 by the Nationalgalerie in Berlin), never became part of his collection.[15] Nevertheless, Lewin's villa inspired other art collectors from Silesia. For example, when Max Silberberg moved from Beuthen to Breslau in 1920, he commissioned a famous artist—Art Nouveau designer and architect August Endell, who presided over the Art Academy in Breslau after Hans Poelzig's departure in 1918—to decorate the interiors of his villa at Kleinburgestrasse. In addition, Gustava and Alois Landerer, devoted art collectors and friends of Max Slevogt, hired artist Bruno Paul to redecorate their estate at Kaiser-Wilhelm-Strasse 182.

[13]   Karl Scheffler, Breslauer Kunstleben, in: Kunst und Künstler, issue 21, 1923, pp. 111–133.

[14]   Der Tierbildhauer August Gaul, edited by Ursel Berger, Berlin, 1999, p. 58.

[15]   In 1927 due to financial difficulties Lewin decided to sell a big part of his collection at the auction house he knew very well: Cassirer in Berlin. Sammlung Leo Lewin Breslau. Deutsche und Französische Meister des XIX. Jahrhunderts. Gemälde, Plastik, Zeichnungen. Paul Cassirer und Hugo Helbing, Berlin, 1927. Other auctions followed at Paul Graupe in Berlin in 1930 and Rudolph Lepke in Berlin in 1932 (mostly drawings and aquarelles by Adolph Menzel).

When the Nazis came to power, the Lewin family decided to emigrate. Thanks to Leo's contacts in the horse-breeding community he had many friends in the United Kingdom. In 1935 extortionate taxes were levied on German Jews, Lewin was forced to sell part of his art collection for well below its market value in a "Jewish auction" at the Max Perl auction house in Berlin.[16] By then he had no doubt that he could no longer run his business in Germany. After a couple of visits to Great Britain with his wife, Helen, the couple ultimately decided to live in the Durham area, in the northeastern part of the country. By the time they boarded a ship in Bremen to leave Germany on January 27, 1939, a fraction of Lewin's collection—including drawings by Max Liebermann and Adolph Menzel—had already been shipped ahead to their new home.[17] The big pieces of furniture designed by Kaufmann and stained glass windows by Cesar Klein must have been very important to the Lewins as they were not left behind. The collector surely feared what would happen with the sequestrated works of art, whose creators were treated with contempt by the Nazi regime. Kaufmann, who was a Jew, fled to Hungary and somehow managed to avoid the mass deportations to the concentration camps. Cesar Klein's Expressionist style was considered degenerate by the Nazi authorities and as a result he was forbidden to either paint or teach. Klein's paintings, along with those by other artists whom Lewin admired, were included in the infamous exhibition of "degenerate art" presented by the Nazi Party in Munich in 1937. Two months after Leo Lewin fled Germany, the government burned more than 4,000 such pieces in Berlin.

In a bitter twist of history,[18] the emptied villas that had once belonged to some of Breslau's most prominent Jewish families were later taken over by the Nazi authorities. Starting in 1933, Breslau's mayor, Helmut Ribnitzky, lived in the house of the Neissers and Lewin's villa was occupied by the Luftwaffe, while Max Silberberg's house served as a base for the security service of the National Socialist German Workers Party (NSDAP). The home of Carl Lewin was at first taken by the district mayor, Josef Schönwälder, and then in 1941 by Karl Hanke, the fanatical "Hangman of Breslau." As *Gauleiter*, or party leader, of the regional branch of the NSDAP, of Lower Silesia, Hanke was in charge of co-ordinating the deportation of the Silesian Jews to the Theresienstadt ghetto in German-occupied Czechoslovakia and to the extermination camps in the East. Close relatives of Lewin who had remained in Germany after 1939 were exterminated there, including his sister, Cäcilia Markus, who was killed in Auschwitz in 1944. A year earlier, Lewin's younger sister, Johanna Schlamm, was killed by the Gestapo in Berlin.

Although Leo Lewin managed to escape in time, his financial troubles and the Nazification of Germany thwarted his attempt to create a modern temple of art that would long endure; its short-lived existence earned him practically no recognition. Still, even if his artistic choices fail to consistently align with modern tastes, the ambition of his undertaking is deserving of appreciation. Not only is he to be praised for engaging such talented artists to design interiors perfectly suited for presenting his superb art collection, but the creation of this prime example of a *Gesamtkunstwerk*, revered by the art critics of the time, was accomplished within just a few years.

---

[16]   The auctions took place on September 24 and 25, 1935.
See http://www.landesarchiv-berlin.de/php-bestand/arep243-04-pdf/arep243-04.pdf (last accessed March 19, 2025).

[17]   At the end of 1938 Nazi authorities made an appraisal of Leo Lewin's property in Breslau. There were no art pieces mentioned.

[18]   The city was the site of the Jewish Theological Seminary, built in 1854 as one of the first modern rabbi seminaries in Europe and whose first director, Zecharias Frankel, is credited as the principal founder of conservative Judaism.

THE ORNAMENT OF OUR TIMES[1]

Paul Zucker

Reacting to that indifferent, artistically lifeless act of emulating the historical styles that were dominating the production in architecture and decorative arts between 1840 and 1890, an absolute formal purism began first in England and later more intensively in Germany. By avoiding any kind of decoration, proclaiming an unconditional factual and purposive style, designers avoided the use of dated ornaments, in reality a masquerade, to express new content—after all, this was only a negation. From an evolutionary point of view, precluding any final appraisal, functionality turned into pedantry and *Materialgerechtigkeit* (truth to material) into boredom, to anyone seized by a lively feeling for art.

Thirty years prior to the beginning of this new movement, Gottfried Semper had already established his rational concept of style, a term in the field of aesthetics, as well as the Marxist terms in the field of economics—a concept that can only be explained as the result of an encroachment of a scientific and materialist mindset into the humanities. As almost always during the development of the history of ideas, it took only one generation to trivialize and render implicit the intellectual thought of one individual, by which it was diluted and popularized by the German masses.

What was to be a mere reaction, a hefty swing of the pendulum of historical development towards the opposite direction, turned into more than an episode of art historical development, a steady state

condition. This lack of creative power found an elaborate network of aesthetic laws and demands which suspected abundance and brilliance as being reactionary and was frowned upon in an almost dogmatic way. Like today, an incapacity of draftsmanship, reaching for expressionist forms, discredits this healthy and legitimate art form before a broader audience incapable of differentiating them. Henry van de Velde's experiment, the artificial soup of a new naturalistically motivated design, had failed; a feeble and unruly Post-Rococo had failed to elevate the language of his lines to pathos.

For almost 15 years, we have detected no attempts of formal progress. Undoubtedly the taste and feeling for proportion are being sharpened. Brutal distortions of proportions are slowly recognized as embarrassing, and the pretentious pathos of gloomy monumentality in the realization of bourgeois interiors and furnishing starts to become more rare. However, now as before, there is a lack of invention or creative power shaped by naïvete. An epoch which employed Impressionism for its pictorial characteristics, which in itself was deeply bourgeois, unemotional, and rationalistic, could produce no other applied art, no other architecture but that which is designed for purpose and practicality.

As it did 20 years earlier, painting and graphic arts sparked a new development. Here new forces struggled first for adequate expression. Now the rational concept of utility could not and was not allowed to be the prime criterion of an architec-

[1] Published in Innendekoration, 1919, pp. 134.

tural creative force. The painter now strives to abstract from the appearance of things, to unveil the essentials of his time, seeing in shape and color the medium which holds the once found expression of this essence. There, the architect and craftsman may straddle their artistic intentions above logic and also manifest a purposeful scheme that is unobjectionable. However, the extent to which this more transcendental artistic will shall find its spatial expression through the creation of architecture will not be examined at this point. For the decoration of the surface, for the culture of the ornamental, it plainly means salvation and resurrection! The cut cord will be tied up again, carefully, and perhaps sometimes with blunder, and the abandoned tradition will be continued. The acanthus leaf, a symbol for a senile academic style from 10 years ago, is no longer relevant. For one was perhaps monumental and generous, perhaps true and honest in this just-past epoch of artful creation, but every organ for the fine, for the delicate in the visual, every feeling for the impact of detail had been totally lost. And, if by 1890, the actual "art" had been stifled by details, and by bad and misunderstood details, then the next 20 years had all too thoroughly eradicated any sense of small-scale effects.

Can we now go further and speak more about a new ornamental content? Is this just a revitalized love for certain old forms or is a new form of ornament being created immediately following a period of lying fallow?

The answer to the question cannot be said with certainty in this sense or the other. In my opinion,

209   Eduard Pfeiffer, carved wall plate, Innendekoration, 1919

contrary to the Jugendstil experiments and Neo-Vienna movement, this time we are in fact dealing with something fundamentally new. Jugendstil and Neo-Vienna believed most of all that they would prove their originality through a radical break with tradition. It is fortunate that the current movement is not as radical in its beginnings, but this very fact makes it more genuine and original. Stylistic traditions, which appear heterogeneous in time and location, have been picked up and spun further. While Neo-Vienna repeatedly modifies only two forms, the heart shape and the bellflower shape, an endless abundance of shapes is now spreading. While further developing flat neoclassical antique basic forms (meander, palette, volute), we recognize the entire wealth of East Asian motifs. Rococo, the main factor in this perception, has provided us with Chinese figures, parrots, pagodas, little bridges, clouds, reeds, herbage, and so on, and by the same intention, certain Assyrian Babylonian and Byzantine stimulations are applied.

The peculiarity of this new stylistic ornament cannot be defined precisely—only perhaps described: at its best one could mention the zigzag, hasty, turbulent rhythm of single shapes harmoniously composed on the surface through an architectonic partition that operates in grand curves and geometric figures. That said, this can only serve as a description and hint—a review of this new ornamental creation as published in the annual volumes of this magazine can explain more than words. For the graphic arts, an especially new moment comes in addition: the "diction," the lines of the ornament, is by all means willful, differing from everything earlier, derived from the works' expressionism. I mean, the unique way to translate linear and flat ornamental motives into drawing can be perhaps understood at its best as an attempt to dynamically exaggerate the lines: the single form, the leaf and the vine is depicted towards one side with hard-edged outlines. The internal values then dissipate from the edge towards the center and are increasingly treated lightly, cloudy, softer and brighter. These bright and airy light surfaces, sweeping into precise curves, consolidate and darken wherever they are crossed by other forms. In other areas, however, particularly striking, significant details seem to radiate a brighter glow around themselves that destroys forms. Almost all new ornamental posters, announcements, book covers, et cetera demonstrate this special feature, through a gradual increase in the expressiveness of the line to the highest point—a tight kind of radiation. Here it seems to also be a sign of honest, inner novelty in the shaping of ornament as well as in the synthetic variations of the historic range of shapes mentioned above.

As a parallel to this new ornamental conviction, a modified position towards the material can be understood in its the development in the years leading up to the war. After overcoming the period of zinc cast and mahogany-like stained pine boards, the principle of *Materialgerechtigkeit* was dogmatized to such an extent that even those techniques of refinement used at all times of the blossoming arts were eliminated. Snobbish exaggeration of this altogether healthy principle saw in *stucco lustro*[2] the forbidden copying of fine marble stones, and in plaster the condemned imitation of stonemason-like surface treatment, among others. However, not every refinement technique that tries to achieve the effect of a nobler one with an inferior-quality material can be accused of deliberate plagiarism. Similarity to the artistic result does not equate to pretense of material identity. Therefore, because of this deliberate limitation, we were deprived of many stimulating and enriching effects. First and foremost this resulted in the use of few and oft-repeated woods, metals, and stones. This uniformity of the material was one of the main reasons for this stylistic humdrum into which the development at last had led. With enthusiasm we were finally allowed in recent years to observe the use of exquisite and manifold fabrics; to recognize how to get new appeal out of long-known woods with new stains; to forge new technologies expanded on formal possibilities of smithery, and so on. The newly acquired enrichment in substantiality worked naturally to form further development.

In this sense the form of expressions could be perhaps determined, which began to develop the feeling for fineness and delicacy of the ornamental form in the years just before the war. The question that remains to be answered now is whether we are only dealing with a developmentally isolated incident, which remained without consequences, like an island in the (the sea of) historical events. Has this progression been cut off and killed because of the war and the economic conditions? I believe—

[2]   Plaster technique.

210　Eduard Pfeiffer (March 4, 1889–October 21, 1929),
stucco design, Innendekoration, 1919

in the keenest opposite to every materialistically determined economic concept of history—that such shaping tendencies, once born out of a national psychological situation, while just following intrinsic laws, are having an impact regardless of any outer occurrences inherent to material things. Therefore I am convinced that the regained joy for the ornamental, especially in an epoch such as we are facing, will live on and live up to its full intensity. Perhaps the range of its applicable field may be limited, perhaps or for sure the upcoming social upheaval will imply an extensive standardization of types for interiors, furniture, and articles of daily use in every sense. Thus the new power of design will be limited in its applicability to just exquisite objects but it will never be repealed. And even then there will be vast areas of artistic creativity, within

which the use of certain ornamental shaping will not be obliged to an economic increase in output. It does not matter to the production costs of a book cover or a poster whether the surface is ornamentally filled or simply framed by straight lines. This relative freedom from economic conditions applies not only to graphic arts but also to textile design, to wallpapers, decorative painting, as long as it will be executed with stencils and so on, in short, for all those areas of decorative design on which a once established design can be mechanically reproduced. But also ornamental blacksmiths, stonemasons, cabinetmakers and architects will still be able, even under the tightest economic budgets, to treat single specially accented surfaces ornamentally. Artistic activity in this new sense, in the feeling of our time, remains for us a possibility!

211   Eduard Pfeiffer, bedroom for Alexander Koch,
Deutsche Kunst und Dekoration, 1917

212   Eduard Pfeiffer, armoire of the bedroom in fig. 211,
Deutsche Kunst und Dekoration, 1917

213   Carved panel of armoire in fig. 212,
Innendekoration, 1914

THE SERPENT CHANDELIERS
BY BRUNO PAUL

Michael Mertens

214   Bruno Paul (January 19, 1874–August 17, 1968),
ceiling chandelier, brass, circa 1913, private collection

Bruno Paul enriched and shaped the early modern period after Art Nouveau from 1905 with his solid, classicism-inspired furniture designs. These designs consistently feature a clear tectonic structure.

Known as the "Master of Linear Style,"[1] Paul is especially recognized for his "Typenmöbelpro-gramm," a standardized furniture program that embodied the principles of the German Werkbund in terms of craftsmanship and serial production.

In his interiors, Paul complemented his rational furniture with playful elements that manifested in textiles, wallpapers, curtain and upholstery fabrics, metal fittings, and particularly lighting fixtures. The textiles predominantly feature abstract geometric patterns. It is striking that in these accompanying decorations, Paul rarely worked with figurative or zoomorphic motifs, especially given that his artistic development began with drawings for the magazines *Jugend* and *Simplicissimus*, which were always figurative and often caricatured.

---

[1]   Sonja Günther, Bruno Paul, 1874–1968, Berlin, 1992.

Exceptions to the geometric decor are large-scale floral-patterned fabrics and, between 1910 and 1925, a series of ceiling chandeliers and wall fixtures that use the motif of the serpent. In these chandeliers, serpents form the arms of the fixture, which are grouped around a spherical center.

From contemporary publications and preserved examples, five basic types of serpent chandeliers can be identified.

All are made of solid brass or bronze, demonstrating substantial material weight. Each individual element and its assembly exhibits the highest precision. All parts are specially designed and manufactured; no mass-produced or purchased elements, including chains or canopies, are used.

Variations within the basic types include the number of chandelier arms, the design of the suspension using chains or rods, and the incorporation of dividing intermediate elements like funnels, flower cups, spheres, or disks, as well as surface treatments that may be blackened, gilded, or silver–plated.

The arms are narrower and more abstracted than naturalistic serpent bodies. They are modeled with subtle swellings, which formally express the inherent static forces. Consequently, they have a vertically elongated oval cross-section to avoid any impression of sagging. As taut lines, they connect the principles of Art Nouveau by Henry van de Velde with classical tectonics, which applies optical corrections such as entasis, the swelling or bulging of the column shaft. Thus, these serpent bodies are not imitations of nature but ideal forms of the tensed muscular power of an erecting body, shaped with organic regularity. The concluding heads bring the form to a calm horizontal finish that can securely balance the mounted light source. The five basic types, which I will refer to as A through E, differ in size, shape, and construction of the central elements and the positioning of the adjacent arms.

TYPE A
WALL AND CEILING CHANDELIERS FROM 1910 ONWARDS

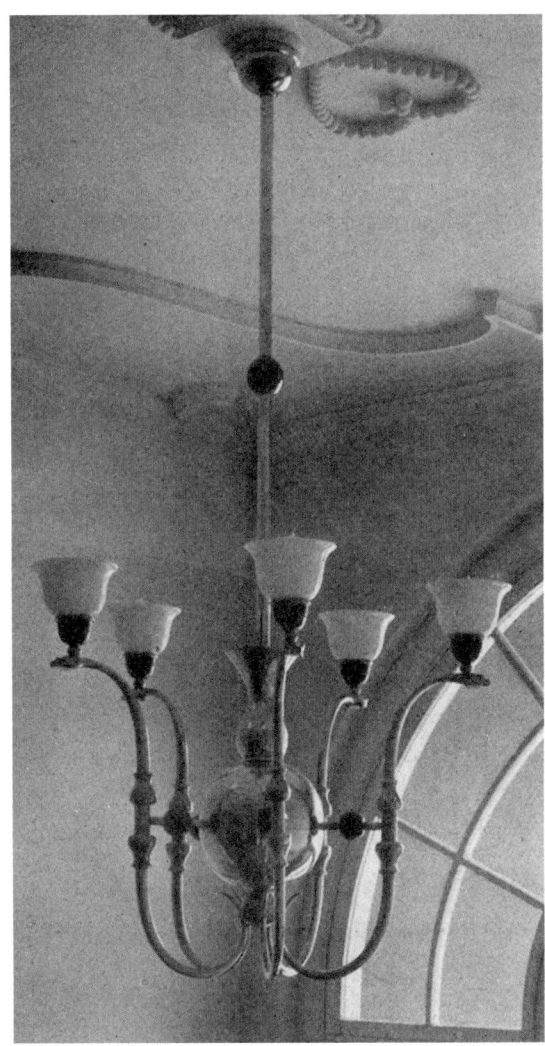

215   Ceiling chandelier in the upper staircase of the Herz house, Berlin, 1913/14

This very elegant five-armed chandelier is known exclusively from the Herz house in Berlin, which was built by Paul in 1913/14. Its classification as the earliest type is due to the fact that a pair of three-armed wall sconces, closely related to it, was already displayed in the exhibition rooms of the Vereinigte Werkstätten in Berlin in 1910. Below the central sphere, the snakes begin an upward movement, lifting their heads to the height of a crowning flower cup. About halfway up, the arms are anchored to the central structure by struts reinforced with spheres, counteracting the tendency of the steeply rising bodies to tilt and thereby achieving a harmonious balance of opposing forces.

The heart-shaped cuffs encircling the snakes above and below the struts can be interpreted, along with the ceiling stucco ornamentation, as a reminiscence of the owner family, Herz.

216   Wall sconce VW 16427 near the fireplace of a hall in the exhibition rooms of the Vereinigte Werkstätten für Kunst im Handwerk in Berlin, 1910

TYPE B
CEILING CHANDELIERS
FROM 1912 ONWARDS

217   Ceiling chandelier VW 16041 in the Hainerberg house, Königstein, 1912

This chandelier follows the reverse principle, with eight serpents curving downwards and closely embracing the dominant, large central ellipsoid body, though held at a distance by spheres strung on intermediate rods about halfway up. They originate from above the central body, which is weighted by another ellipsoid, crowned with a sphere. The overall impression exudes Baroque opulence.

The model is exclusively known in an eight-armed version and was used by Bruno Paul in 1912 in the residential hall of the Hainerberg house for the Frankfurt industrialist Adolf Gans in Königstein im Taunus, and in the office of the Cologne tobacco merchant Joseph Feinhals. It also hangs in the study of the house built by Peter Behrens for the archaeologist Theodor Wiegand in Berlin-Dahlem. The chandelier Type B was cataloged as model 16041 by the Vereinigte Werkstätten.

TYPE C
WALL AND CEILING CHANDELIERS
FROM 1913 ONWARDS

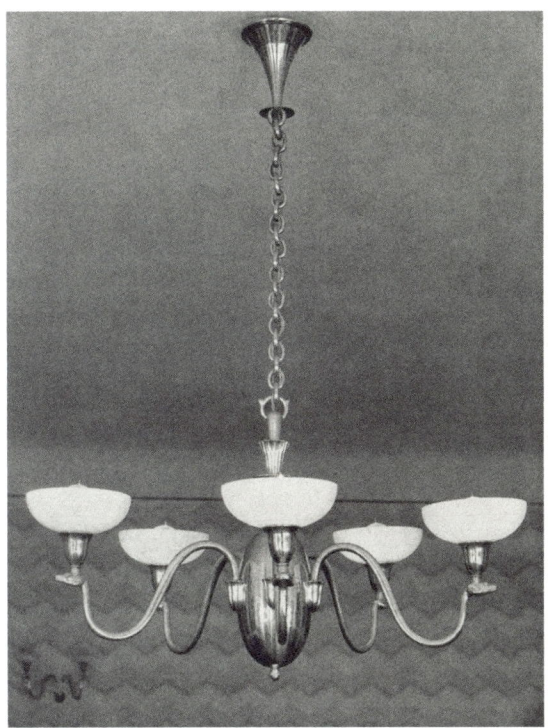

218   Ceiling chandelier, 1913, private collection

own study, as well as for clients such as Röchling, Leitz, Sobernheim, and Piesbergen over a period of approximately 10 years. In 1915 Paul Mebes used a similar piece in a conference room of the Nordstern Insurance Company in Berlin.

Two-armed wall sconces complemented the ceiling crown in the hall of the Sobernheim family's Waltrud house on Schwanenwerder Island, as well as in the showrooms of the Zoo-Werkstätten in Berlin.

Contemporary literature from 1924 identifies the Vereinigte Zoo-Werkstätten Berlin, which only came into existence in late 1923,[2] as the manufacturer of a chandelier with Type C wall sconces.

Three five-armed and one seven-armed ceiling chandeliers, as well as one wall sconce, are known to be in private collections. Another seven-armed chandelier has been located in the hall of Dr. Leitz's Villa Friedwart by Bruno Paul in Wetzlar since its construction in 1917.

The chandelier arms, which can be read as snake bodies, are only partially visible in this type. Instead, they emerge from a basket-like half-shell attached laterally to the ellipsoidal central body. For ceiling chandeliers, this half–shell is ribbed, while for wall chandeliers, it is smooth with a finishing bead.

Since the snakes on this chandelier can extend elegantly in an S-shape due to the lateral starting point, this design achieves a particularly generous harmony. The diameter with five arms is 88 cm, and with glass shades, it measures 96 cm. Paul used the chandelier in a seven-arm version in his

219   Wall sconce, brass, circa 1913, private collection

---

2   Alfred Ziffer, Bruno Paul, Munich, 1992, p. 102.

TYPE D
CEILING CHANDELIERS
FROM 1921 ONWARDS

Paul used this fixture in 1921 in the Fränkel house in Hamburg, as reported in the publication *Deutsche Kunst und Dekoration* from July 1923. In 1924, it was featured in *Innendekoration* with a reference to the manufacturer Vereinigte Zoo-Werkstätten Berlin. It also appeared again in the 1925 exhibition at the Richmodishaus in Cologne. The diameter is 92 cm, and with glass shades it measures 110 cm. One example exists in a private collection.

220 Ceiling chandelier, circa 1921, private collection

The central ellipsoid in this type is compressed and topped with a tall cone and a subsequently placed floral cup. The serpents extend above the central body, curling to a point as they cling to it and the cone.

222 Ten-arm ceiling light, Gerson Exhibition, 1924

221 Light fixture, living room of Landhaus Fränkel, Hamburg, circa 1921

The ten-arm configuration, as seen in the Sternberg house in Soest and also known from the exhibition rooms of Fa. Gerson in Berlin and the Richmodis hause in Cologne, represents a return to the early Type A. It achieves this by adding five more upward-reaching arms between the five original arms of the base type, alternating them.

The motif of the struts positioned between the serpents and the central body is a reprise of earlier models. The composition exhibits an exceptional tension due to the precision of contrasting horizontal, vertical, and curved elements.

TYPE E
CEILING LIGHT FIXTURES
FROM 1922 ONWARDS

The light fixtures with snake arms were used exclusively in Paul's interiors for living halls and studies, where a uniform, glare-free illumination provided by the glass shades was required. These were occasionally complemented by wall, floor, or desk lamps.

For the study of the archaeologist Theodor Wiegand, a heavy snake chandelier (Type B) by Paul was chosen. This is surprising because the architect of the house was Peter Behrens, not Bruno Paul.

223 Light fixture, circa 1922

224 The Wiegand house, men's study, circa 1913

This light fixture varies the principle of freely extending snake arms by incorporating the stereometric forms of the 1920s, such as spheres, cylinders, and hemispheres, instead of the oval forms of the 1910s.

The fixture is not attributed to any specific installation by Bruno Paul. It was exhibited in the *Deutsche Gewerbeschau* in 1922, indicating that it was available for the public to purchase.

The diameter measures 70 cm; with glass shades 78 cm. Two known examples exist, one in the Munich Stadtmuseum and one in a private collection.

Behrens designed not only the chandeliers but also the entire furnishings for the other main rooms.

The study is defined by its extensive library cabinets, which, along with a writing and discussion table, form the infrastructure supporting the homeowner's passion for archaeology. As such, it was likely the most personal of the main rooms, and it seems plausible that this chandelier was installed at the request of the homeowner, Wiegand. His fascination with Orientalism beyond Roman-Greek antiquity, which is hinted at in Behrens's classical design, may have been stirred by this object, which exudes an undefined exoticism. This ambiguity is evident when examining other rooms designed by Paul

225   The Sobernheim house, fireplace area in the hall,
circa 1913

Archaeology," both founded in 1906. Paul likely followed their excavations under the leadership of Ludwig Borchardt, culminating in the discovery of the bust of Nefertiti in 1912.

Thus, the symbolic meaning of the serpent as a "bearer of light" seems to have provided Paul with an attractive basis for his design of modern light fixtures. With this, he was able to present his clients with a metallic, sparkling sculpture that, aside from fulfilling its functional purpose, poetically conveyed the idea of protecting the dwelling and its inhabitants with the eternal radiance of the sun.

from the early 1910s. Some of these rooms feature design elements derived from Egyptian culture. For instance, the fireplace wall of the hall in the Sobernheim house, flanked by snake chandeliers, is complemented by a stuccoed papyrus frieze reminiscent of the capitals of the columns from the Temple of Kom Ombo. The temple is adorned with numerous depictions of uraeus serpents, which typically emerge in pairs from a central cartouche.

The uraeus serpent is regarded in Egyptian mythology as a protective deity of the Pharaoh. In this role, it is depicted as carrying the sun disk on its forehead. With this light, it drives away darkness, symbolically representing Egypt's enemies. Pharaohs, therefore, have worn this serpent symbol on their headdresses since the Middle Kingdom. It also appears on furniture, such as the throne of Tutankhamun, or as architectural decoration, as seen in Kom Ombo.

Through his close acquaintance with Wilhelm von Bode, the director of the Königliche Museen zu Berlin, whose influence led to Bruno Paul's appointment in 1906 as director of the Kunstgewerbemuseum, Paul would have been aware of the development of the "German Oriental Society" and the "Imperial German Institute for Egyptian

226   Uraeus fitting from shrine, cupreous metal,
Egypt, 664–630 BCE,
The Metropolitan Museum of Art,
New York, inv. no. 41.160.110

227   Unknown, light fixture, carved walnut,
western Germany, circa 1920

228   Fritz A. Breuhaus, detail of the chest in fig. 232

FURNITURE
IN THE EXPRESSIONIST
ROCOCO STYLE

Markus Winter

At the beginning of the 20th century, the number of styles available to the designer of a home was seemingly unlimited. They ranged all the way from Assyrian to Cubist. This eclecticism was very much in the spirit of Ulrich, the protagonist from the novel *The Man Without Qualities* by Robert Musil,[1] who seeks to find order in extremes. As a reader, my three favorite examples of this strategy are the following: first, the relationship between the mucous membrane of the lips and that of the intestine; the second, the trajectory from conception to suicide; and the third, the chasm between racial mixing and segregation.

But Musil poses a fourth and final opposition through Ulrich's experience: the radical difference between life in the country and life in the city. He can no longer return to country life because he has lost what Musil calls "the primitive epic to which private life still clings, although in public, life can no longer be narrated." The thread of heroic narrative has snapped, leaving existence "to spread out, in an infinitely interwoven surface."[2]

In citing Musil's oppositions, I wish to establish that the furniture discussed here, which falls outside the construction of the "modern," was in fact the very pulse of the 1910s and 1920s. Musil's musings on the "primitive" bookend this article. The furniture at hand not only is evidence of a particular style, but also moves towards a specific cultural horizon. The primitive has been invented by a society that fears being primitive. The scope of this article, however, is limited to examining a type of furniture that embodies a fearlessly cosmopolitan persuasion, not a social critique.

For the architect and art historian Paul Zucker (1888–1971), no one style can be better or worse than any other, for the very nature of styles is comparative rather than progressive.[3] Wilhelm Pinder (1871–1947) goes further, asserting that there had never been an orderly historical enfilade of styles.[4] Progress, when speaking of design, is merely an academic fantasy that has trickled down to the collective. Instead of a distinct transition from one style to the next, and to the next style after that, style engulfs us in a tidal wave. The Central European architects working from 1910 to 1930 lived out a highly energized dialectic between what may simplistically be called the linear and the painterly, or the static and dynamic.[5]

---

[1]   Robert Musil, Der Mann ohne Eigenschaften, Hamburg, 1952, p. 20.

[2]   Ibid., p. 665.

[3]   Paul Zucker, Styles in Painting, New York, 1963, p. 6.

[4]   Wilhelm Pinder, Die deutsche Plastik vom ausgehenden Mittelalter bis zum Ende der Renaissance, Berlin, 1914, p. 119.

[5]   Heinrich Wölflin, Kunstgeschichtliche Grundbegriffe, Munich, 1915.

The essence of Expressionist Rococo is movement, especially if we consider Oscar Kaufmann to be the main exponent, if not inventor, of the style. The term "Expressionist Rococo" was used in 1928 by Oscar Bie[6] and Max Osborn[7] to describe the work of Kaufmann, who was primarily a theater architect.

Rococo is one of several stylistic antecedents of Expressionism as it has existed through the ages. During the same decade that Rococo and Expressionism diverged, a new type of entertainment architecture was emerging, especially in Berlin. In 1913, the year in which the story of *The Man Without*

229   Unknown, commode, polychrome-decorated and parcel-gilt, Potsdam, 1700–1720, Galerie Neuse, Bremen

230   Hugo Pál, foyer at the Marmorhaus, murals and stained glass by Cesar Klein, Berlin, Deutsche Kunst und Dekoration, 1913

Nine years earlier, both words had appeared separately in an article about the new ornamental creations of Paul Zucker.[8] Zucker particularly praised Rococo of the 18th century because it drew so exuberantly upon the "whole treasure trove of East Asian motifs." At the same time, he lauded Expressionism, for its "peculiar way of graphically reproducing linear and two-dimensional ornamental motifs—best understood, perhaps, as an attempt to augment the dynamic language of lines."[9]

Qualities begins, the Marmorhaus on the Kurfürstendamm was completed according to the designs of the Hungarian architect Hugo Pál. This movie theater was described in the magazine *Kunst und Dekoration* as an Indokino, "in which the decoration smelled like the jungle of the Ganges." The article goes on to say that the wall paintings by Cesar Klein were depictions of hashish dreams. The foyer ceiling, festooned with gathered fabric, was compared to a monumental jupon, or ruffled underskirt. Beneath this ceiling was a table resembling an Indian altar.[10] A period photograph reveals all these individual elements synthesized in a landscape of exotic styles.

6   Oscar Bie, Der Architekt Oskar Kaufmann, Berlin, 1928.

7   Max Osborn, Oskar Kaufmann, Berlin, 1928.

8   Paul Zucker, Das neue Ornament, in: Innendekoration, 1919, p. 134.

9   Ibid., p. 172.

10   Rudolph Töpfer, Ein neues Lichtspielhaus in Berlin, Deutsche Kunst und Dekoration 1913, p. 433.

The Chinese House in Potsdam (1755–1764), a masterwork of the Rococo of Frederick the Great, also exhibits a combination of ornaments from distant continents. Life-sized Chinese figures inhabited a pavilion inflected with Egyptian detail, notably in the oval windows of the roof, adorned

231   Fritz August Breuhaus
(9 February 1883–2 December 1960)
lady's room in the architect's city apartment,
Cologne, Innendekoration, 1921

with scarablike muntins. Like Frederician architecture, the furniture of his period became an important source of inspiration for Berlin in the 1910s and 1920s. Lucian Bernhard erected altars on chests of drawers and secretaries Baroque in style as elements of his interiors.

Prior to 1910, Oskar Kaufmann's furniture was still cubic and static. Only the marquetry on his cupboards was designed with forceful diagonals, reminiscent of the veneer patterns of architect Paul Ludwig Troost (fig. 51). During Kaufmann's interior design of Villa Leo Lewin (1917–1921), ornamentation which in 1910 appeared almost as an afterthought to decorated cubic forms was replaced by a basic Baroque form already defined by the plans. The curvaceous front legs of the dining room chair for Villa Levin may be compared to the legs of a dresser by Michael Hoppenhaupt (1685–1751). While Hoppenhaupt's legs still taper slightly

towards the ground, the termination of Kaufmann's leg seems to sink into the ground.

Like Kaufmann, Leo Nachtlicht (1872–1942) also adapted the language of the Rococo. S-shaped curved frames and protruding corners are

232   Fritz August Breuhaus, chest with one drawer and one flap, lacquered wood, circa 1920, private collection

reminiscent of a corner cabinet at Potsdam made of cedar wood attributed to Georg Wenzeslaus von Knobelsdorff (1699–1753), or of Johann Melchior Kambly's (1718–1783) tortoiseshell furniture for Frederick the Great. The upper ends of the mirrored hutches, their segments tapering at acute angles, echo the basic shape of console table tops designed by Nachtlicht (fig. 97). Neither Nachtlicht nor Kaufmann followed such historical inspirations to the letter, but rather reinvented them to express their own, or sometimes the frenzied, zeitgeist. If you compare Nachtlicht's dressing table with the Kambly desk, the new, cheeky freedom of modernity seems quite evident. While the décor in Villa Schwalbe (1925) was accentuated with silver, it is very likely that the ornaments on the table illustrated here were not separated by color. Like

233   Walter Würzbach (August 1887–May 3, 1971),
bedroom for Wolfgang Gurlitt, murals by Cesar Klein, *Danae* bed relief by Rudolf Belling,
Wasmuths Monatshefte für Baukunst, 1921, Bildarchiv Foto Marburg

splashes of paint in a grisaille, the carvings are part of the composition.

Along the spectrum of inspirations they shared, neither Kaufmann nor Nachtlicht limited themselves to the German style or tradition. The Italian, French, and Bohemian Baroque, notably the pilgrimage church of St. John of Nepomuk at Zelená Hora by Santini Aichel—based on the pentagram—were directly quoted.

In my view, however, within Expressionist Rococo, a certain "German-ness" resurfaces in the wild streak that defines the Baroque. Art historian Paul Ferdinand Schmidt (1878–1955) perceived the gradual loss of this "Germanic" essence in the wildness of 17th-century Baroque.[11]

I would like to illustrate another Berlin project as a salient comparison: the furnishings for Wolfgang Gurlitt, shown in *Wasmuths Monatshefte für Baukunst* in 1921. Walter Würzbach is named as the designer, the wall paintings were done by Cesar Klein, and a sculptural work ornamenting the bed was created by Rudolf Belling. Whereas Belling's sculpture is applied to the foot of the bed, decorative applications to the dressing table and side table are inseparable from the structure or base. The table tops still bear a traditional profile but are now incised with large, machine-like grooves, and the base is designed like a talus. The S-shaped center leg is a profile that, so to speak, decorates itself.

There are occasional flashes of wildness in the designs of Fritz August Breuhaus de Groot and Emil Fahrenkamp, who worked between Berlin and the Rhineland. Breuhaus, who added de Groot to his

---

[11]   Paul Ferdinand Schmidt, Der Pseudoklassizismus des 18. Jahrhunderts, in: Monatshefte für Kunstwissenschaft,
vol. 8, issue 10, 1915, p. 372.

234 Leo Nachtlicht (August 12, 1872–September 22, 1942),
lady's room in the house of Dr. Schwalbe,
Innendekoration, 1922

last name in the late 1920s, initially mixed heavy Baroque fantasy furniture with Czech Cubism and provincial farmhouse types. For example, he applied ornaments and profiles to the basic shape of a Piedmontese Madia—a trunk for bread dough and other foods. Borrowing from the concept of the *figura serpentinata*, the shafts of floor lamps (fig. 38) literally wind their way up from heavy carved plinths to the illuminating bulb. The torsion itself becomes a metaphor for life's tensions and resolutions, offering profound insights into the human condition, particularly in the context of the wound—physical, emotional, and spiritual—and its potential for transformation. Fahrenkamp, in turn, imposed Gothic arches on cupboards (fig. 132) or tapered mirrors (fig. 56). Like Bruno Taut's celebrated pavilion of colored glass, Fahrenkamp's spires seem to connect to an unknown higher realm.

All that was foreign was perceived by these designers to be so remote and strange as to embody "the unknown," both temporally and geographically. Eduard Pfeiffer's work in particular was characterized by Fritz Ostini as "strange," in the journal *Innendekoration*: "He puts the romantic, the fairy-tale, and fantastic alongside the most primitive and simple designs, with an artistry at once rich and self-sufficient, naive and well-versed in everything beautiful from the past. Pfeiffer fears the accusation of being archaic, just as little as he deserves it."[12] Ostini continues: "Relief figures flank a coat of arms, a dancer with tambourines, and a violinist. The whole fantasy of Pfeiffer's ornamental style is concentrated in these figures. Headdresses and robes are from no time or place. The whole conception of the figures is foreign—and naive—things audaciously created by an idiosyncratic and powerful imagination—but strange."[13]

---

[12] Fritz Ostini, Eine Neue Arbeit Eduard Pfeiffers, in: Innendekoration, issue 7/8, 1919, p. 220.

[13] Ibid., p. 229.

236　Eduard Pfeiffer, lady's room in the house of Erich Ferdinand Laeisz, Deutsche Kunst und Dekoration, 1924

235　Eduard Pfeiffer (March 4, 1889–October 21, 1929), drawing for a collector's cabinet, circa 1920, Germanisches Nationalmuseum, Nuremberg

Kaufmann, too, absorbed foreign influences, embodying Karl Friedrich Schinkel's assertion that "the influences of foreign nations are only healing if they are received with prudence; only then do they have their true effect by merging with our own characteristics."[14] This approach is evident in the furniture at Villa Lewin, adorned with figures that evoke both European folkloric dancers and African sculptures. In the dining room, however, Kaufmann followed a more classical precedent, blending these influences seamlessly with tradition. Here, hidden on the inside of cabinet doors, intarsia pictures depict the wine, women, and song of the Dionysus cult. On the dining room chairs, a sea shell like the Venus clam surmounts the backrest, not unlike Chippendale.

Kaufmann's furniture can thus be read on different planes. It possesses on the one hand the dialectical Dionysian-Apollonian narrative; on the other, it represents with grandeur the social aspirations of the Levins. Folkloric references, African forms, and traces of Italian antiquity comfortably cohabit, belying the essential radicalism of the design. Greek and Egyptian antiquity abide under one roof with Central European folklore, along with so-called 'primitive' designs. Beneath the formality of style circulates the mythical content of ritual, which, as art historian and curator Rolf Wedewer (1932–2010) notes, "is peculiar to both the modern and the primitive."[15]

In 1864, architect Edwin Oppler (1831–1880) called for new synagogues to be built in the "German" style.[16] Kaufmann, however, preferred to propagate a style that paid homage to the world's diverse cultures and drew inspiration from festivals,

14　Alfred von Wolzogen, Aus Schinkel's Nachlaß, vol. 3, Berlin, 1863, p. 159.

15　Rolf Wedewer, Form und Bedeutung: Primitivismus, Moderne, Fremdheit, Cologne, 2000, p. 98.

16　Edwin Oppler (1864), quoted in Harold Hammer-Schenk, Edwin Opplers Theorie des Synagogenbaus, in: Hannoversche Geschichtsblätter, vol. 32, issue 1–3, 1979, p. 106.

237   Eduard Pfeiffer, detail of an ivory intarsia for a cabinet, Museum für Kunst & Gewerbe, Hamburg

238 | 239 Otto Firle (October 14, 1889–July 4, 1966), commode, lacquered and gilt wood, marble top, manufactured by Deutsche Holzkunst-Werkstätten Johannes Andresen A.G., Bremen, circa 1923, Wright Auction, Chicago

games, and ceremonies. The Expressionist Rococo of Kaufmann and his colleagues drew both praise and criticism. Contemporaries such as the urban theorist Marcello Piacentini (1881–1960) published a photograph of Kaufmann's showroom for the Bechstein piano company.[17] An Orpheus and the Animals spiral staircase, based on Kaufmann's design, is shown next to a stark Constructivist drawing of a Russian propaganda project, with a horizontally mounted cylinder and a vertical cube defining its thrust. After World War II, architects such as Carlo Mollino (1905–1973), Andrea Busiri Vici (1903–1989), and Michele Busiri Vici (1894–1981) continued to incorporate Baroque and Expressionist Rococo forms into their work.

17 Marcello Piacentini, Architettura d'oggi, Rome, 1930.

Bibliography

Adam, Hans Christian, Karl Blossfeldt. The Complete Published Work, Cologne, 2014

Anderson, Stanford/Grunow, Karen/Krohn, Carsten, Jean Krämer. Architekt / Architect, Weimar, 2015

Ay, Andreas, Neues Wohnen in alten Mauern, Lich, 2012

Baldacci, Paolo/Schmied, Wieland, Die andere Moderne. Giorgio de Chirico und Alberto Savinio, Ostfildern, 2001

Barovier, Marino, et al., Vittorio Zecchin 1878–1947. Pittura, vetri, arti decorative, Venice, 2002

Bauhaus-Möbel, A Legend Reviewed, Bauhaus Archiv, Berlin, 2002

Beardsley, Aubrey/Wilde, Oscar, Salome, New York, 1967

Benton, Charlotte/Benton, Tim/Wood, Ghislaine (eds.), Art Deco. 1910–1939, London, 2003

Berents, Catharina, Art Déco in Deutschland. Das moderne Ornament, Frankfurt am Main, 1997

Berger, Ursel (ed.), Der Tierbildhauer August Gaul, Berlin, 1999

Bie, Oscar, Der Architekt Oskar Kaufmann, Berlin, 1928

Billeter, Erika, et al., Die Zwanziger Jahre. Kontraste eines Jahrzehnts, Bern, 1973

Bilski, Emily/Bauschinger, Sigrid (eds.), Berlin Metropolis. Jews and the New Culture. 1890–1918, Oakland, 2000

Boccioni, Umberto, Pittura e scultura futuriste. Dinamismo plastico, Milan, 1997

Boehm, Gottfried, Canto d'amore, Bern, 1996

Brandenburg, Museums, https://brandenburg.museum-digital.de/

Brandstätter, Christian, et al., Design der Wiener Werkstätte 1903–1932, Vienna, 2003

Brett, David, On Decoration, Cambridge, UK, 1992

Breuer, Gerda, et al., Bauhaus Conflicts 1919–2009. Controversies and Counterparts, Berlin, 2010

Breuhaus, Fritz August, Das Haus in der Landschaft, Stuttgart, 1926

Breuhaus, Fritz August, Bauten und Innenräume, Charlottenburg, undated (circa 1921)

Breuhaus, Fritz August, Landhäuser und Innenräume, Düsseldorf, 1911

Brittain-Catlin, Timothy, Double Deutsch, in: The World of Interiors, London, 2019, pp. 182–189

Calloway, Stephen, Twentieth-Century Decoration, New York, 1988

Campbell, Joan, Der Deutsche Werkbund. 1907–1934, Stuttgart, 1981

Christie's, sale 15785, The Collection of Paul F. Walter, New York, 2017

Conrads, Ulrich (ed.), Die Bauhaus-Debatte 1953. Dokumente einer verdrängten Kontroverse, Braunschweig, 1994

Dekorative Kunst, Munich, 1900–1929, https://www.digitale-sammlungen.de/en/dekorative-kunst/items

Deutsche Illustrierte Rundschau, Munich, 1924–1932

Deutsche Kunst und Dekoration, Darmstadt, 1897–1932, https://nbn-resolving.org/urn:nbn:de:bsz:16-diglit-63833

Dexel, Grete/Vitt, Walter/Dexel, Walter (ed.), Der Bauhausstil. Ein Mythos, Starnberg, 1976

Duncan, Alastair, Art Déco. Die Epoche, die Künstler, die Objekte, Munich, 2009

Ecke, Gustav, Chinese Domestic Furniture, Vermont, 1962

Eggeling, Tilo, Raum und Ornament, Regensburg, 2003

Einstein, Albert/Freud, Sigmund, Warum Krieg?, Dijon, 1933

Fries, Herbert de, Moderne Villen und Landhäuser, Berlin, 1925

Galerie Jacques de Vos, Eileen Gray, Paris, 2014

Galerie Neuse, L'apothéose du génie, Bremen, 2019

George, Stefan, Das Jahr der Seele, Berlin, 1929

Giedion, Sigfried, Space, Time and Architecture. The Growth of a New Tradition, Cambridge, MA, 1941

Glaeser, Ludwig, Ludwig Mies van der Rohe. Furniture and Furniture Drawings, New York, 1977

Groom, Gloria Lynn, Gauguin. Artist as Alchemist, Chicago, 2017

Günther, Sonja, Bruno Paul. 1874–1968, Berlin, 1992

Gurlitt, Cornelius, Die Baukunst Konstantinopels, Berlin, 1907/1912

Guttry, Irene de/Maino, Maria Paola, Andrea Busiri Vici. Architetto (1903–1989), Rome, 2000

Guttry, Irene de/Maino, Maria Paola, Il mobile italiano degli anni '40 e '50, Bari, 1992

Guttry, Irene de/Maino, Maria Paola, Il mobile deco italiano. 1929–1940, Bari, 1988

Hambrock, Heike, Bauen im Geist des Barock. Hans und Marlene Poelzig, Berlin/Delmenhorst, 2005

Hammer-Schenk, Harold, Edwin Opplers Theorie des Synagogenbaus, in: Hannoversche Geschichtsblätter, vol. 32, issues 1–3, 1979, pp. 101–117

Handler, Sarah, Austere Luminosity of Chinese Classical Furniture, Berkeley, 2001

Hanenberg, Norbert, lecture: Eduard Pfeiffer. Ein Dichter unter den Architekten, Germanisches Nationalmuseum, Nuremberg, 2022

Hänsel, Jessica, et al., Baumeister – Ingenieure – Gartenarchitekten, Berlin, 2016

Hansen, Antje, Oskar Kaufmann. Ein Theaterarchitekt zwischen Tradition und Moderne (Die Bauwerke und Kunstdenkmäler von Berlin), Berlin, 2001

Harrison, Stephen/Coffin, Sarah D./Orr, Emily M., Jazz Age. American Style in the 1920s, Cleveland, 2017

Hersey, George L., The Lost Meaning of Classical Architecture, Cambridge, 1988

Herzogenrath, Wulf (ed.), Die Deutsche Werkbund-Ausstellung Cöln 1914, Cologne, 1984

Heuter, Christoph, Emil Fahrenkamp 1885–1966. Architekt im rheinisch-westfälischen Industriegebiet, Petersberg, 2002

Hillier, Bevis, Art Deco of the 20s and 30s, London, 1968

Hoeres, P., Der Krieg der Philosophen. Die deutsche und britische Philosophie im Ersten Weltkrieg, Paderborn, 2004

Hoff, August, Emil Fahrenkamp, Stuttgart, 1928

Hoffmann, Tobias, Deutschland gegen Frankreich. Der Kampf um den Stil 1900–1930, Cologne, 2016

Hung, Jochen, Beyond Glitter and Doom. New Perspectives of the Weimar Republic (H-Soz-u-Kult: Tagungsberichte, 2010), Munich, 2012

Huth, Martha, Berliner Lebenswelten der zwanziger Jahre. Bilder einer untergegangenen Kultur, Frankfurt am Main, 1996

Innendekoration, Darmstadt, 1900–1944, https://nbn-resolving.org/urn:nbn:de:bsz:16-diglit-67100

Jacobson, Dawn, Chinoiserie, New York, 1999

Jenkins, Palden, http://www.palden.co.uk/

Johnson, Paul, The Birth of the Modern, New York, 1991

Junger, Ernst, In Stahlgewittern, Stuttgart, 2001

Juranek, Christian, Art Déco. Kunst des Historismus? (Edition Schloß Wernigerode, vol. 22), Wettin-Löbejün, 2019

Kaufhold, Enno, Berliner Interieurs. Photographien von Waldemar Titzenthaler (1910–1930), Berlin, 1999

Keun, Irmgard, Das kunstseidene Mädchen, Berlin, 1932

Keyserling, Hermann, Der Sinn der Persönlichkeit, in: Innendekoration, Darmstadt, 1927, pp. 82–84

Kirichenko, Evgenia, Russian Design and the Fine Arts 1750–1917, New York, 1991

Kisluk-Grosheide, Daniëlle/Krohn, Deborah L./Leben, Ulrich, Salvaging the Past. Georges Hoentschel and French Decorative Arts from The Metropolitan Museum, The Bard Graduate Center, The Metropolitan Museum, New Haven, 2013

Kisluk-Grosheide, Daniëlle/Koeppe, Wolfram/Rieder, William, European Furniture in The Metropolitan Museum of Art. Highlights of the Collection, New Haven, 2006

Kjellberg, Pierre, Art Déco. Les maîtres du mobilier, le décor des paquebots, Paris, 1986

Koch, Alexander, Farbige Wohnräume der Neuzeit, Darmstadt, 1926

Koch, Alexander, Das neue Kunsthandwerk in Deutschland und Oesterreich unter Berücksichtigung der Deutschen Gewerbeschau München 1922, Darmstadt, 1923

Koch, Alexander, Handbuch Neuzeitlicher Wohnungskultur. Das Vornehm-Bürgerliche Heim Neue Folge, Darmstadt, 1922

Koch, Alexander, Handbuch Neuzeitlicher Wohnungskultur. Herrenzimmer Neue Folge, Darmstadt, 1921

Koch, Alexander, Handbuch Neuzeitlicher Wohnungskultur. Speise-Zimmer, Darmstadt, 1920

Koch, Alexander, Handbuch Neuzeitlicher Wohnungskultur. Das Vornehm-Bürgerliche Heim, Darmstadt, 1917

Koizumi, Kazuko, Traditional Japanese Furniture, Tokyo, 1986

Kolb, Eberhard, Die Weimarer Republik, Munich, 2009

Kopplin, Monika, Gerard Dagly, Munich, 2015

Kracauer, Siegfried, Das Ornament der Masse. Essays, Frankfurt am Main, 1977

Kreisel, Heinrich/Himmelheber, Georg, Die Kunst des deutschen Möbels. Möbel und Vertäfelungen des deutschen Sprachraums von den Anfängen bis zum Jugendstil, Munich, 1968–1983

Krenzlin, Ida Luise, Die mit den Möbeln malte, in: B History. Das Berliner Geschichtsmagazin, issue 4, 2022, pp. 50–57

Kubisch, Sabine, Das Alte Ägypten. Von 4000 v. Chr. bis 30 v. Chr., Wiesbaden, 2017

Kushner, Marilyn Satin, The Art of Winold Reiss. An Immigrant Modernist, New York, 2021

Lagerfeld, Karl, German House, Göttingen, 1998

Landeshauptstadt Hannover (ed.), Hannoversche Geschichtsblätter, Hannover, 1898–

Latour, Alessandra, Louis I. Kahn. Writings, Lectures, Interviews, New York, 1991

Laudert, Doris, Geschichte – Brauchtum – 40 Baumporträts, Munich, 2004

Ławicka, Magda, Miśnieńskie kafle we Wrocławskim muzeum, in: Świat Kominków, issue 4, 2016, pp. 92–94

Leuth, Karl, Wand und Deckendekoration, Leipzig, 1928

Maibaum, Katrin/Gräber, Katharina, Wenzel Hablik. Expressionistische Utopien. Malerei, Zeichnung, Architektur, Munich, 2017

Mandelbaum, Howard/Myers, Eric, Screen Deco, New York, 1985

Meier-Graefe, Julius, Entwicklungsgeschichte der modernen Kunst, Munich, 1966

Moderne Bauformen. Monatshefte für Architektur und Raumkunst, Stuttgart, 1902–1932, https://nbn-resolving.org/urn:nbn:de:bsz:16-diglit-207250

Musil, Robert, Der Mann ohne Eigenschaften, Hamburg, 1952

Nachtlicht, Leo, Olbrich und Messel, in: Velhagen & Klasings Monatshefte, vol. 24, issue 2, October 1909, pp. 201–208

Nerdinger, Winfried (ed.), 100 Jahre Deutscher Werkbund. 1907–2007, Munich, 2007

Neumeyer, Fritz, Mies van der Rohe. Das kunstlose Wort, Munich, 1986

Noever, Peter/Mattl, Siegfried (eds.), Der Preis der Schönheit. 100 Jahre Wiener Werkstätte, Ostfildern, 2003

Noever, Peter, Die Überwindung der Utilität. Dagobert Peche und die Wiener Werkstätte, Ostfildern, 1998

Nüßlein, Timo, Paul Ludwig Troost (1878–1934), Cologne, 2012

Ocón Fernández, María, Ornament und Moderne. Theoriebildung und Ornamentdebatte im deutschen Architekturdiskurs (1850–1930), Berlin, 2004

Olbrich, Joseph Maria, Ideen Von Olbrich, Stuttgart, 2012

Olivier-Vial, Franck/Rateau, Francois, Armand Albert Rateau, Paris, 1992

Oncken, Alste, Friedrich Gilly. 1772–1800, Berlin, 1981

Osborn, Max, Der bunte Spiegel, Louisville, 2013

Osborn, Max, Oskar Kaufmann, Berlin, 1928

Ostini, Fritz von, Das Landhaus "Sankt Antonius." Ein Künstlertraum, Darmstadt, 1918

Ottomeyer, Hans, Empire Style. The Hôtel de Beauharnais in Paris. The German Ambassador's Residence in Paris, edited by Jörg Ebeling/Ulrich Leben, Paris, 2016

Ottomeyer, Hans, Die Erfindung des style Empire, in: König Lustik!? Jérôme Bonaparte und der Modellstaat Königreich Westphalen, edited by Michael Eissenhauer, Kassel, 2008, pp. 53–58

Palica, Magdalena, Von Delacroix bis van Gogh. Jüdische Kunstsammlungen in Breslau, in: Jüdisches Leben zwischen Ost und West. Neue Beiträge zur jüdischen Geschichte in Schlesien, edited by Anno Herzig, Göttingen, 2014, pp. 390–406

Palica, Magdalena, Od Delacroix do van Gogha. Żydowskie kolekcje sztuki w dawnym Wrocławiu (From Delacroix to van Gogh. Jewish Collections of Art in Breslau), Wrocław 2010

Paretzer Skizzenbuch. Bilder einer märkischen Residenz um 1800, Munich, 2000

Paul Cassirer und Hugo Helbing, Sammlung Leo Lewin Breslau. Deutsche und Französische Meister des XIX. Jahrhunderts, Berlin, 1927

Pehnt, Wolfgang, Expressionist Architecture, New York, 1973

Pevsner, Nikolaus, Pioneers of Modern Design, New York, 1986

Philippe, Eric, Collection 10, Paris, 2003

Piacentini, Marcello, Architettura d'oggi, Rome, 1930

Pinder, Wilhelm, Die deutsche Plastik vom ausgehenden Mittelalter bis zum Ende der Renaissance, Berlin, 1914

Pinkham, Roger, Oliver Messel, London, 1983

Pohl-Weber, Rosemarie (ed.), Rudolf Alexander Schröder Wohnräume und Möbel, Bremen, 1979

Popp, Joseph, Bruno Paul, Munich, 1916

Posener, Julius, Berlin auf dem Wege zu einer neuen Architektur. Das Zeitalter Wilhelms II., Munich, 1979

Reifferscheidt, Fabian, Spiritueller Funktionalismus. "Form und Kultus," in: Deutschland gegen Frankreich. Der Kampf um den Stil 1900–1930, Cologne, 2016, pp. 176–183

Rheinheimer, Vivian J., Herbert M. Gutmann. Bankier in Berlin, Bauherr in Potsdam, Kunstsammler, Leipzig, 2007

Roh, Franz, Nach-Expressionismus. Magischer Realismus. Probleme der neuesten europäischen Malerei, Leipzig, 1925

Rüger, Maria (ed.), Ernst Barlach. Werke und Werkentwürfe aus fünf Jahrzehnten, Berlin, 1981

Schäche, Wolfgang/Szymanski, Norbert, Paul Zucker. Der vergessene Architekt, Berlin, 2005

Scheffler, Karl, Breslauer Kunstleben, in: Kunst und Künstler, issue 21, 1923, pp. 111–133

Scheper, Renate, Farbenfroh! Die Werkstatt für Wandmalerei am Bauhaus / Colourful! The Wallpainting Workshop at the Bauhaus, Bauhaus Archiv, Berlin, 2005

Schmidle, Elisabeth, et. al., Fritz August Breuhaus 1883–1960. Kultivierte Sachlichkeit, Tübingen, 2006

Schmitz, Hermann, Berliner Baumeister vom Ausgang des achtzehnten Jahrhunderts, Berlin, 1914

Schmitz, Hermann, Deutsche Möbel d. Klassizismus, Stuttgart, 1922

Schneider, Katja, Paul Thiersch und die Bühne. Szenische Visionen eines Architekten, Halle, 1995

Schrader, Bärbel/Schebera, Jürgen, Golden Twenties, New Haven, 1988

Schreyer, Alexander, Die Möbelentwürfe Johann Michael Hopfenhaupts des älteren und ihre Beziehungen zu den Rokokomöbeln Friedrich des Grossen, Strassburg, 1932

Sievers, Johannes, Schinkel. Die Möbel, Berlin, 1950

Sildatke, Arne, Dekorative Moderne. Das Art Déco in der Raumkunst der Weimarer Republik, Berlin/Münster, 2013

Sotheby's, The Collection of Count and Countess Volpi di Misurata – Palazzo Volpi Unveiled, Paris, February 28, 2024

Steiner, Rudolf, Bausteine zu einer Erkenntnis des Mysteriums von Golgatha, Dornach, 1996, GA 175

Steiner, Rudolf, Das Verhältnis der verschiedenen naturwissenschaftlichen Gebiete zur Astronomie, Dornach, 1997, GA 323

Stiftung Brandenburger Tor, Harry Graf Kessler. Flaneur durch die Moderne, Berlin, 2016

Stolarska-Fronia, Małgorzata, Jewish Art Collectors from Breslau and their Impact on the City's Cultural Life at the End of the 19th and the Beginning of the 20th Century, in: Jüdische Sammler und ihr Beitrag zur Kultur der Moderne, edited by Annette Weber, Heidelberg, 2011, pp. 237–253

Stratigakos, Despina, Hitler at Home, New Haven, 2015

Thun-Hohenstein, Christian/Thun-Salm, Christiane/Boeckl, Matthias/Witt-Dörring, Christian, Josef Hoffmann, Adolf Loos. Wege der Moderne und die Folgen / Ways to Modernism and Their Impact, Basel, 2015

Ulmer, Renate, Emanuel Josef Margold, Stuttgart, 2003

Varia, Radu, Brancusi, New York, 2002

Vegesack, Alexander, Czech Cubism. Architecture, Furniture and Decorative Arts, New York, 1992

Venturi, Robert, Learning from Las Vegas, Cambridge, 1977

Villa Grisebach, auction no. 217, Berlin, November 28, 2013

Votteler, Arno, Wege zum modernen Möbel. 100 Jahre Designgeschichte, Munich, 1989

Warhaftig, Myra, Deutsche jüdische Architekten vor und nach 1933. Das Lexikon. 500 Biographien, Berlin, 2005

Wasmuth, Ernst, Wasmuths Monatshefte für Baukunst, 1914–1931

Wedewer, Rolf, Form und Bedeutung. Primitivismus, Moderne, Fremdheit, Cologne, 2000

Die Weltkunst, Hamburg, 1930–

Wichmann, Siegfried, 20er Jahre. Drei Künstler: J. Wackerle, E. Pfeiffer, A. P. Nestler, Engelhorn-Stiftung, Munich, 1977

Wilfinger, Laura, "My home is my castle" oder Brecht an Bord der Bauhaus?, in: An Bord der Bauhaus. Zur Heimatlosigkeit der Moderne, edited by Sonja Neef, Bielefeld, 2009, pp. 57–74

Williams, Kandis (ed.), Josephine Baker. Icon in Motion, Cologne, 2024

Wilton-Ely, John/Eisenman, Peter, Piranesi as Designer, New York, 2007

Wolf, Max, Die Milchstrasse und die kosmischen Nebel, Potsdam, 1925

Wölflin, Heinrich, Italien und das deutsche Formgefühl, Munich, 1931

Wölflin, Heinrich, Kunstgeschichtliche Grundbegriffe, Munich, 1915

Wölflin, Heinrich, Prolegomena zu einer Psychologie der Architektur, Munich, 1886

Wolzogen, Alfred von, Aus Schinkel's Nachlaß. Reisetagebücher, Briefe und Aphorismen, vols. 1–3, Berlin, 1862–1863

The World of Interiors, London, 1981–

Ziffer, Alfred (ed.), Bruno Paul. Deutsche Raumkunst und Architektur zwischen Jugendstil und Moderne, Munich, 1992

Zinutti, Lucien, Il linguaggio del mobile antico, Treviso, 2011

Zucker, Paul, Fascination of Decay, Ridgewood, 1968

Zucker, Paul, Styles in Painting, New York, 1963

Zucker, Paul, Die Theaterdekoration des Barock, Berlin, 1925

Heiko Adrian, Berlin: Fig. 204

Archive Böttcherstraße, Bremen, photo: Rudolph Stickelmann: Fig. 84

Dawo Auction, Saarbrücken: Fig. 203

Detroit Institute of Arts: Fig. 53 (Acc. no.: 01.4)

Francis Dizikowski: Fig. 115

Espace Emmanuel Eyraud, Paris: Fig 190

Foto Archiv Marburg: Fig. 233 (fm83429)

© Fotostudio Bartsch, Karen Bartsch, Berlin: Fig. 198

Don Freeman: Figs. 16, 17, 20, 22, 24, 25, 26, 29, 31, 33, 35, 36, 38, 39, 41, 43, 44, 45, 47, 48, 49, 50, 51, 57, 58, 60, 61, 63, 69, 71, 72, 73, 75, 77, 79, 90, 93, 94, 96, 97, 99, 101, 105, 113, 114, 116, 117, 119, 120, 135, 136, 142, 143, 145

Friedrich Wilhelm Murnau Foundation, Wiesbaden: Figs. 4, 138

Galerie Neuse, Bremen: Fig. 229

Germanisches Nationalmuseum, Nuremberg: Figs. 74 (GNM, DKA, NL Pfeiffer, Eduard, 49), 76 (GNM, DKA, NL Pfeiffer, Eduard, Mappe 8–V [3]), 235 (GNM, DKA, NL Pfeiffer, Eduard, Mappe 13a, Teil III)

The Metropolitan Museum of Art, New York: Figs. 2 (# 2004.363.1), 95 (# 1975.101), 150 (# 1989.197), 226 (# 41.160.110)

Museum of Modern Art, New York: Fig. 6 (USA, Scala, Florence, Pencil on paper (29.7 x 21 cm). Mies van der Rohe Archives, gift of the architect, Acc. no.: 926.1974)

Max Villani: Fig. 13

Markus Winter: Figs. 1, 8, 9, 11, 14, 15, 55, 56, 66, 80, 81, 82, 83, 86, 87, 88, 91, 103, 106, 107, 108, 109, 110, 122, 123, 125, 129, 130, 133, 134, 139, 140, 141, 144, 148, 149, 152, 153, 154, 159, 161, 162, 164, 165, 166, 169, 170, 171, 174, 175, 175, 176, 184, 187, 192, 197, 201, 202, 205, 214, 219, 220, 227, 228, 232, 237

Wright Auction, Chicago: Figs. 238, 239 From the collections of Schloß Wernigerode GmbH, photo: Michael Lumm: Fig. 7 (Gr.000416)

FROM PUBLICATIONS

Bie, Oscar, Der Architekt Oskar Kaufmann: Figs. 27 (pl. 61), 54 (pl. 102), 179 (col. pl. I), 200 (pl. 66), 206 (pl. 65), 207 (pl. 50), 208 (pl. 55)

Bruckmann, Die Kunst, Munich: 222 (1918, p. 96)

Dekorative Kunst: Figs. 19 (1920, issue 3, p. IV), 92 (1917, vol. XXV, p. 128), 111 (1925/26, vol. XXXIV, p. 165), 189 (1912, vol. XX, p. 81), 194 (1913, vol. XXI p. 308)

Deutsche Illustrierte Rundschau: Fig. 98 (1927, p. 853)

Deutsche Kunst und Dekoration: Figs. 3 (1921–1922, vol. XLIX, p. 56), 30 (1920–1921, vol. XLVII, p. 79), 32 (1908, vol. XXI, p. 125), 42 (1927–1928, vol. 61, p. 227), 46 (1914, vol. XXXIV, p. 223), 52 (1911, vol. XXVIII, p. 37), 62 (1930, vol. 66, p. 59), 78 (1914–1915, vol. XXXV, p. 139), 126 (1920–1921, vol. XLVII, p. 336), 146 (1917–1918, vol. XLI, p. 51), 147 (1914, vol. XXXIV, p. 356), 156 (1923, vol. 53, p. 43), 157 (1910–1911, vol. XXVII, p. 335), 158 (1919–1920, vol. XLV, p. 353), 160 (1919–1920, vol. XLV, p. 372), 163 (1911, vol. XXVIII, p. 275), 211, 212 (1917, vol. XXXIX, pp. 407, 411), 215 (1920, vol. XLVI, p. 328), 216 (1911, vol. XXVIII, p. 115), 218 (1924, vol. 54, p. 169), 221 (1923, vol. 52, p. 240), 225 (1919, vol. XLIV, p. 44), 230 (1913, vol. XXXII, p. 437), 236 (1924–1925, vol. 55, p.82)

Innendekoration: Figs. 18 (1909, vol. XX, p. 17), 21 (1921, vol. XXII, p. 258), 34 (1921, vol. XXXII, p. 358), 37 (1921, vol. XXXII, p. 222), 40 (1922, vol. XXXIII, p. 230), 59 (1937, vol. XLVII, p. 40), 64 (1912, vol. XXIII, p. 47), 65 (1924, vol. XXXV, p. 382), 85 (1926, vol. XXXVII, p. 212), 100 (1922, vol. XXXIII, p. 146), 132 (1923, vol. XXXIV, p. 131), 151 (1914, vol. XXV, p. 430), 155 (1926, vol. XXXVII, p. 31), 167 (1920, vol. XXXI, p. 395), 172 (1924, vol. XXXV, p. 223), 173 (1928, vol. XXXIX, p. 488), 177 (1922, vol. XXXIII, p. 40), 178 (1922, vol. XXXIII, p. 37), 183 (1927, vol. XXXVIII, p. 305), 195 (1911, vol. XXII, p. 307), 209, 210 (1919, vol. XXX, p. 135), 213 (1914, vol. XXV, p. 448), 224 (1913, vol. XXIV, p. 444), 231 (1921, vol. XXXII, p. 199), 234 (1922, vol. XXXIII, p. 147)

Koch, Alexander, Das neue Kunsthandwerk: Fig. 223 (p. 145)

Koch, Alexander, Farbige Wohnräume: Fig. 70 (p. 91)

Leuth, Karl, Wand und Deckendekoration: Fig. 102

Moderne Bauformen: Figs. 10 (1912, p. 90), 12 (1910, p. 621), 67 (1928, pl. I), 68 (1929, p. 302), 104 (1912, pl. 78), 118 (1928, pl. 13), 121 (1922, p. 278), 124 (1923, pl. 10), 137 (1922, p. 244), 168 (1926, p. 370), 180 (1932, pl. 8), 181 (1926, pl. 18), 182 (1927, pl. 47), 186 (1922, pl. 73), 188 (1917, pl. 5), 191 (1914, pl. 21), 193 (1914, p. 456)

Oncken, Alste, Friedrich Gilly. 1772–1800: Fig. 5 (p. 52)

Osborn, Max, Oskar Kaufmann: Fig. 89 (pl. 51)

Paretzer Skizzenbuch: Fig. 112 (Fol.: 6)

Popp, Joseph, Bruno Paul: Fig. 217 (p. 179)

Regione Lombardia: Fig. 131 (https://www.lombardiabeniculturali.it/fotografie/schede-complete/IMM-3u030-0015155)

Schreyer, Alexander, Die Möbelentwürfe Johann Michael Hoppenhaupts des älteren: Fig. 28 (p.I)

Sievers, Johannes, Schinkel: Fig. 128 (fig. 48)

Wasmuths Monatshefte Für Baukunst: Figs. 185 (1921, vol. VI, 7/8), 196 (1925), 199 (1922/23, p. 335)

Wikipedia: Fig. 127 (https://en.wikipedia.org/wiki/Gro%C3%9Fes_Schauspielhaus#/media/File:Berlin_Grosses_Schauspielhaus_Poelzig_Foyer.jpg)

Ziffer, Alfred, Bruno Paul: Fig. 23 (p. 262)

Every effort has been made to trace copyright holders and obtain permission for the use of images. If, despite these efforts, any rights have been overlooked, the publisher is prepared to make the necessary corrections in subsequent editions.

© 2025 Markus Winter, Don Freeman, the authors, and arnoldsche Art Publishers, Stuttgart

Editors
Don Freeman, Markus Winter

Authors
Ulrich Leben, Michael Mertens, Magdalena Palica, Arne Sildatke, Markus Winter, Paul Zucker

Copy editing
Wendy Brouwer, Stuttgart

Graphic designer
Piotr Bondarczyk, New York

Printed by
GPS Group

Paper
Munken Polar Rough 120 gsm

Bibliographic information published by the Deutsche Nationalbibliothek
The Deutsche Nationalbibliothek lists this publication in the Deutsche Nationalbibliografie; detailed bibliographic data are available at www.dnb.de.

Cover illustrations
Front: Detail of a two-door sideboard in fig. 154
Back: Two-door sideboard in fig. 154

This book has been produced with the generous support of:

Raquel Nicolas, Lux Winter, Christiane Schaath, Lisa Stamm, Hildegard Schulte, Chelsey Mitchell, Milena Neermann, Dani Fer Oz, Amanda Powell Walker, Helene Close, Danica Cosic, Marie Saeki, Cate Corcoran, Andrea Mitchell, Larilyn Sanchez, Olga Granda, Harley Wertheimer, the Carmichaels, Erin Knight, Robin Miller, Samantha Spencer, Sarah Charbonneau, Elle Dalton, Juhee Kimura, Brian Wilson and Tony Hale, Adam Lippes, Sean O'Hara, C. Michael Diaz, Brian Kish, Michael Jefferson, Charles Sailey, Mark Andrews, David Bogoslaw, Alex Poston, Garrett Swanson, Andy Rifkin, Fernando Santangelo, Isaiah Whisner, Hugo Rossi, Lasse Hynninen, James Harrison, Matthew Benjamin, Ulrich Feldhahn, Kevin A. Hunter, Jonas Gaupp, Matthew Lyons, Ryan Lawson, Adam Charlap Hyman, Fabio Olivotti, Sascha Kuhlmann, Peter Langh, Michael Mertens, Alexej Koschkarow, Stefan Kruger, Jürgen Zauner, Gregory Gilmartin, Silard Isaak, Alexander Edwards, Robert Allen Fairbairn IV, Henrik Langsdorf, Alastair D. Taylor, Kurt Johann Klemm, Matteo, R. Louis Bofferding, Clark Giles, Alan R. Murdoch, Doug Meyer, Henny, Saved New York Inc.

mobile Gesellschaft der Freunde
von Möbel- und Raumkunst e.V.

ISBN 978-3-89790-741-6
Made in Europe, 2025